NINE MIRACLES

WHEN BULLETS CAN'T KILL AND HOPE PREVAILS

BRODY YOUNG AND AUSTIN MURPHY

Radius Book Group
New York

Radius Book Group
A division of Diversion Publishing Corp.
www.radiusbookgroup.com

Copyright © 2025 by Brody Young and Austin Murphy

All rights reserved, including the right to reproduce this book or portions thereof in any form whatsoever. No part of this publication may be reproduced or transmitted in any form or by any means, electronic or mechanical, including photocopying, recording, or any other information storage and retrieval, without the written permission of the publisher.

Radius Book Group and colophon are registered trademarks of Diversion Publishing Corp.

For more information, email info@radiusbookgroup.com.

The publisher does not have any control over and does not assume any responsibility for author or third-party websites or their content.

First Radius Book Group Edition: June 2025

Book design by Scribe Inc.
Cover design by Elizabeth Kingsbury
Cover photo by Bret Edge Photography and Jaeger Clark Young

Hardcover ISBN: 9781635768732
E-book ISBN: 9781635768756
Printed in the United States of America
10 9 8 7 6 5 4 3 2 1

CONTENTS

FOREWORD by Wendy Young		v
ACKNOWLEDGMENTS		vii
INTRODUCTION: "Only *Mostly* Dead"		ix
1	THE DANCE WITH DANGER	1
2	RUN AT THE FEAR	13
3	"THE COURSE OF TRUE LOVE NEVER DID RUN SMOOTH"	23
4	FROM RIVER GUIDE TO RANGER	39
5	BLINDSIDED	53
6	"NOT ON MY WATCH"	69
7	ALLEN MEMORIAL'S FINEST HOUR	73
8	"IS HE GOING TO DIE?"	81
9	"IF YOU WAKE UP MY KIDS, I'LL KILL YOU"	93
10	"GOD, LIFE FORCE, ENERGY, KARMA"	99
11	NOT OUT OF THE WOODS	107
12	HERE COMES DEBRIDE	119
13	ANGELS APPEAR	127
14	THE "F" WORD	137

CONTENTS

15	WAYBACK MACHINE	149
16	MANHUNT	157
17	ALONG CAME THE SWIRLY	173
18	STRONG AT THE BROKEN PLACES	185
19	SKELETON MAGNET	199
20	MOM POWER	207
21	"WE GOT OUR GUY"	217
	EPILOGUE	233

FOREWORD

Wendy Young

I've always thought that if I wrote about our experiences from 2010, I would title the book *Come Hell or High Water*.

As river guides we lived for high water. We combed weather forecasts and snowpack reports as soon as the season ended each year, hoping that the next would see numbers well over 100 percent!

High-water years are the stuff of legend. Massive waves, gnarly holes, and extreme eddies. Rowing big water is a thrilling, adrenaline-pumping experience laced with sheer terror. There is nothing like it.

And that's how our lives went in 2010. It was epic. Incredible things happened; our lives were forever changed, both by a huge outpouring of good and by some crazy rough bad. It was filled with a whole lot of high water and a wee bit of hell.

ACKNOWLEDGMENTS

There are so many who stepped up and went beyond during our time of need. Gratitude needs to be cultivated and has an extremely positive effect on our vibrational frequency. I declare:

Our Father and His Son.

Wendy, Stryder, Jayde, and Jaeger.

Our Moms and Dads.

Our extended family, whom we love through thick and thin.

Kim, Lindsey, Austin, and Gary. You know!

Thurl Bailey, Robert Patrick, and Howard White.

Jeremy Johnson, who flew his own helicopter during the initial search.

Friends and neighbors who were near and far and the new friends we've gained through this experience.

Those who cared and prayed for us on our behalf. It worked!

Those who organized and attended the benefit fundraiser and other financial efforts on our behalf.

Those who donated blood to my name.

Those around the world who touched our lives for the better.

ACKNOWLEDGMENTS

Lance and his family.

The first responders who answered the call hastily that night and in the following days, named by agency: Department of Natural Resources Utah State Parks; Utah Division of Wildlife Resources; Forestry, Fire and State Lands; Utah Highway Patrol/Special Emergency Response Team (SERT)/K-9; Department of Public Safety's Star 7 Helicopter Unit; Price Dispatch; Utah Attorney General's Office; Grand County Sheriff's Office; Grand County Dispatch; Grand County Emergency Medical Services; Grand County Search and Rescue; Moab City Police Department; Moab Fire Department; San Juan County Sheriff's Office and Emergency Management Team; National Park Service from Canyonlands and Arches; Weber County Sheriff's Office; Carbon County Sheriff's Office and Special Weapons and Tactics Team; Utah County Sheriff's Office Special Weapons and Tactics Team; Adult Probation and Parole; Statewide and Information Analysis Center; Federal Bureau of Investigation; Homeland Security; and the Utah Governor's Office.

To the hospital employees—clerks, janitors, nurses, doctors—at both Allen Memorial and St. Mary's Regional Hospital.

To those who still do good in the world, the peacemakers. And to those who haven't been or aren't yet—you're one step away.

To those I've forgotten, please forgive me. Thank you!

And finally, to all those who have passed away. Our heads are bowed. We will meet again!

INTRODUCTION

"Only *Mostly* Dead"

It happens less frequently as the years roll past, but it still happens. I will stop to help someone in the backcountry of southeastern Utah or pull them over to issue a citation. They'll look at my face for a couple extra beats or notice my name tag, and I'll see in their eyes a flicker of recognition.

Next comes the question, "Are you that guy?" and I will smile and answer, "Yep. I'm that guy." And even if I'm writing them up for speeding or illegal off-roading, the contact takes a friendly turn. Folks ask how I'm doing, and I tell them "Fine" and thank them for asking.

I feel obligated, at that point, to share some details, to recount a miracle or two from the night I should have died but lived.

They drive away with a ticket and a story and, I hope, a bit of inspiration.

I am asked a different question every so often, and the answer is no: I'll never get used to the vistas in this strange and wondrous part of the planet—the red rock and burnt

INTRODUCTION

cliffs and canyonlands around my adopted home of Moab, Utah. It doesn't get old.

I am drawn more powerfully still to the river that carved those canyons: The river that brought my wife and me together as members of the same thrill-seeking tribe, that gave me an income first as a whitewater guide and then as a specialized ranger with the Utah Division of Parks and Recreation.

The river that delivers us to remote and harshly beautiful country, forbidding and unreachable by road, and that gives us solitude and space for reflection and—though less frequently these days—the adrenaline rush of the rapids as we whoop and holler, our throats crowded with joy and just a bit of fear.

The river that rolled mutely past on the night I lay dying a few hundred feet from the water's edge, looking up at the man who'd just fired fifteen rounds at me from his Glock semiautomatic handgun, nine of those .40-caliber bullets striking me—ten if you include the slug that pierced my wallet, tucked in the right-front cargo pocket of my uniform pants.

I was on my back in the dirt of the parking lot at the Poison Spider Mesa trailhead, with no other humans around for miles. I was waiting for the bad guy to finish me off, but he turned away instead, walking back toward his car. In his mind, I think, I was already dead.

It would've been fine by me to avoid that hail of bullets—to mark out the rest of my days blissfully ignorant of how I might handle the adversity of being shot repeatedly and left for dead by a stranger I'd just offered to help.

You wouldn't be reading this book if I hadn't crossed paths with Lance Leeroy Arellano on November 19, 2010. And I wouldn't be walking around with a slug lodged in my spine and another in my hip, another in the lower lobe of my left lung, and still another butting up against the left ventricle of my heart. I wouldn't be missing four feet of small intestine and three feet of my colon (leaving me with, as friends have noted, a semicolon).

As it turns out, I had no choice in the matter. I did, however, have the agency to choose how I would *respond* to that attack. And here, just over five hundred words into this book, we arrive at one of its core messages. Sure, I'll write a lot about steely-eyed surgeons and heroic EMTs and what a straight-up badass my wife is. But the lesson I most want to get across is that all of us are born with this superpower: the ability to choose the way we respond to our circumstances—to adversity.

I could have let go, my lifeblood seeping into the loose gravel of that parking lot. I could have given up the ghost and shuffled to the next realm—to what awaits us at the end of this life.

Or I could fight back.

I now think of that ambush not as something that happened to me but as something that happened *for* me. Arellano was the forty-year-old who shot me in the back after I offered to help him, then kept shooting until he ran out of

INTRODUCTION

bullets. He was also my teacher, underscoring for me the value and importance of training—of practicing, drilling, creating motor memory, respecting and embracing the process, whatever your process may be.

I was an unlikely law enforcement officer, but I took my training seriously. And it was that training that kept me alive long enough to give others—the gallery of guardian angels you'll meet soon enough—the chance to bring *their* training to bear, which ended up saving my life.

It wasn't his intention, but Arellano also ended up highlighting, for me and others, the importance—the primacy—of the bonds we share with those in our families and communities. I've tried to find a less saccharine way to say that. But it's true. When I was bleeding out on the ground, vision narrowing, consciousness fading, what flashed in my mind's eye were images of my wife and our three children. I needed to get back to them. That's the imperative that jump-started me—gave me the strength, the will, the *chi* to start crawling toward my truck, toward the radio that was my sole link to the outside world.

While a lot of Utah is culturally monolithic, Moab is an eclectic outlier. Unlike most cities in this ruby-red state, liberals outnumber conservatives (although it's close). Latter-day Saints (LDS) like me make up just under half of Utah's population but less than 30 percent of Moab's. Old families who've been here since the uranium boom of the 1950s are neighbors with more recent arrivals—arrivistes buying second homes, driving up the price of real estate, and earning

INTRODUCTION

the enmity of that former group. You've got the law enforcement community and the river-guiding community. There are the churchgoers—Protestants, Catholics, Baptists, Episcopalians, and so on in addition to the Latter-day Saints. And there are those for whom the trails and open sky and rock formations are church enough.

"There are a lot of lines drawn in town, a lot of butting heads and groups fighting for this, fighting for that," my friend Merrill Hugentobler once noted. "When this happened," he recalled, referring to the night I got shot, "all that melted away, and it was time to help out Brody and his family."

Not long after I was ambushed, doctors put me in a reversible—a.k.a. "medically induced"—coma that lasted three and a half weeks. Emerging from that deep sleep, I couldn't help but flash back, repeatedly, obsessively, to the attack. I was gripped by an intense, oppressive fear, an anxiety I couldn't escape. During my night terrors in the ICU, I would shout at the specter of a gunman in my mind, thinking I was awakening and unnerving my fellow patients. I was alone in my room.

But I found relief in forgiveness. Lying in a hospital bed, tubes sprouting from me, machines humming and beeping all around, I set vengeance aside. I forgave the man who tried to kill me. I couldn't hate anyone right then. I didn't have the bandwidth. It takes a lot of energy to hate! As soon as I made that conscious decision, I felt a weight lifted, an opening inside. I'd set down a burden, in the process expanding my capacity to heal and experience joy and reclaim my life.

INTRODUCTION

All that sprung from an act of forgiveness.

As I shared with a journalist in 2023, "Lance and I are going to meet again, and it's going to be like water under the bridge. It's not even going to matter. He was going through a bad patch, and I ended up in his crosshairs. I forgive him completely. That's truly how I feel."

What follows is the story of how I survived that attack and what the experience taught me about the value of family and friendships, the power of forgiveness, and the importance of training and trusting your gut. And fighting back.

One of the many doctors I worked with was Robert J. McLaughlin, MD, an occupational medicine physician in Grand Junction, Colorado. He's a guy you go see when you've been injured on the job. Because a big part of his practice is helping patients get back to work, Dr. McLaughlin draws them out on their careers, their families, their relationships. He's a good listener, conversationalist, and storyteller. And he's from New Jersey, which gives him a certain novelty out here in the American West—more so because he embodies a stereotype about folks from back East. He speaks with what I assume is a Jersey accent. And there's a bluntness to him that I find refreshing.

The first time I met him, he motioned to some MRI images of all the new projectiles and fragments in my body. "Why aren't you dead?" he said in the same tone he might have used to ask why I'd chosen chips instead of fries with my BLT. "I can't believe you're not dead." When McLaughlin gets on a roll, he tends to talk faster and sounds like Billy Crystal's

INTRODUCTION

Miracle Max in *The Princess Bride* when he tells Inigo Montoya (Mandy Patinkin), "It just so happens that your friend is only *mostly* dead. There's a big difference between mostly dead and all dead. Mostly dead is slightly alive."

One morning during my convalescence, McLaughlin told me the story of a patient from early in his medical career. He was interning at a hospital in Philadelphia, sitting across from an elderly gentleman who had a kind of aura about him. "I get this patient, this older guy. I'd just met him, but I kept looking at him. Not sure why. And he says, 'Yep, I'm supposed to be dead.'" Twenty years earlier, the man had been diagnosed with some malign, aggressive cancer and told he had only months to live. When McLaughlin asked how he'd cheated death, the man told him, "I just decided, I'm not gonna die. Ain't goin'. Not my time."

At the time, McLaughlin was just out of medical school, his mind steeped in the physiology and pathology of the human body—"at my rational, scientific peak," he says. He shares the story of that defiant old cancer survivor to remind patients and himself "that every day, a doctor somewhere is saying to someone, 'You've only got a few months to live'—and we're totally wrong. It's rare. But we're wrong." Not all medical outcomes can be explained by science. "So there's something else," he concludes.

I'll spend time in these pages exploring that mysterious space and the string of inexplicable events that came together to keep me alive. I'll recount the outpouring of generosity and kindness that followed. *Nine Miracles* is a

INTRODUCTION

reference to the number of bullets that hit me. And one of those miracles must surely be how a single act of evil resulted in so much good.

"I'm Afraid He Would Try to Injure You Guys"

The following is an excerpt from an interview with Lance Arellano's mother, conducted by detectives from the Grand County Sheriff's Office a day after the shooting. She declined our overtures to speak with her. To grant her some measure of privacy, we will not use her name.

DETECTIVE: Tell me honestly, do you like cops?

LANCE'S MOTHER: A few. I was married to a [redacted] cop ... in Salt Lake County.

DET.: So I take that as a no? Or will you give us a fair chance?

LM: I'll give you a fair chance because I want to help my boy. If you get him cornered, you better call [one of his] friends to try to talk him out. 'Cause I don't think he'll believe any of the cops. He hasn't had a very good experience.

DET.: How old is your son, exactly?

LM: He's forty years old.

DET.: He's a person of interest in this thing. We have his car; we have some personal effects in the car that say he was in the car. And everything adds up, but we haven't seen him. And we can't call him a suspect until we verify that that was him at the scene.

If it is your son, he's out in some pretty rough country in some extreme conditions, and he's ill-equipped.

LM: If you find him, you're gonna need his friend to talk him out.

DET.: What would he [Lance] do?

LM: I'm afraid he would try to injure you guys.

DET.: Why?

LM: Because he wouldn't believe you.

Chapter 1

THE DANCE WITH DANGER

When I was eleven, our family moved from West Valley City, Utah, to a house on the outskirts of Mesa, Arizona, not far from the smaller city of Apache Junction, with the stark crags of the Superstition Mountains looming farther to the east.

This high desert country was markedly different from the landscape we'd left—so dramatic it was as if I'd stepped into a Hollywood western. I was quite taken with it, just as I was highly interested in the BB gun owned by one of my new friends. After I asked him a few times, he let me borrow it, and that led to one of the more painful lessons of my young life.

So armed, I ventured into some open space and saw lizards and a few rabbits. But they were wary and quick, and I was no danger to them.

Suddenly I spied a hummingbird hovering between two bushes. I didn't think; I just took aim. In the fraction of a second before I pulled the trigger, the bird turned its head and looked right at me. Stared into my soul. And what did I do? I closed my eyes and shot. I heard a *POW*—BB guns are louder than you think—then a soft thud. Looking down, I saw the lifeless bird, and my heart sank.

I'd never hurt or killed another creature, and now I was suffused with sadness and sharp regret. Nobody was around, so I actually got down on my knees and prayed over the hummingbird, then tried prodding it back to life. I even tried little chest compressions, avian CPR, to no avail.

With my hands I excavated a shallow grave for the bird, then buried it. I returned the BB gun to my friend's house and never fired it again. I circled back to the gravesite the next day, and the hummingbird was gone. I held out fleeting hope that it had somehow sprung back to life and flown away. But even at that tender age, I knew better in my heart of hearts. Some coyote had dug it up and wolfed it down. It made me inexpressibly sad.

I did shoot some slingshots thereafter, but never at a living target. I never wanted to take a life again. Any life. I didn't own a gun until I became a state ranger.

I was born in Idaho, the eldest of the four children of Bruce and Jody Young. At the time, my parents were working as caretakers on the farm of an older couple. I have three younger sisters: Heather, Katie, and Jamie. I kept waiting for Mom to give me a little brother, but he never arrived. So I spent a lot of time pleading with my sisters to throw a ball around with me.

We moved to Utah and then to Arizona in hopes that the warm, dry climate would benefit Mom, who was chronically ill for almost as long as I can remember. Mom passed away in 2000 at the age of forty-seven, a few months after Wendy and I married. She had lupus and spent much of her final decade tethered to a dialysis machine. She was a beautiful, kind soul, and we're grateful she lived to see our wedding.

I was around five when doctors figured out what was making my mom so sick. Lupus turns the body's immune system on itself, tricking it into attacking its own tissues and organs. By the time I was seven, Mom had fallen gravely ill. Her hair was falling out in the sink in clumps. We were searching for any kind of treatment for her, and someone told us about a healer named Iohanni Wolfgramm.

A native of Tonga, Wolfgramm had served the church as a labor missionary, building chapels in the islands before immigrating to Utah in 1965. A high priest in his Salt Lake City ward, he was well known for saving the life of his three-year-old daughter after she was run over by a Jeep.

It was quite a test to believe this man had such a gift—that he'd brought his little girl back from the dead. My father took that leap of faith, desperate like the rest of us for someone to help my mother.

And Wolfgramm did. Almost immediately after he anointed my mom with oil, prayed over her, and gave her his priestly blessing, her lupus went into remission. For months, my mom improved. Her suffering abated. And even though that improvement turned out to be temporary, in the long run, our family has always regarded that event as a miracle. As a young boy I held this belief, stored in a lockbox deep in my heart, that miracles do happen. As a grown man, I owe my life to them.

But the time came, a few years later, when Mom's kidneys had basically shut down. Her reprieve this time was a miracle of science. She was the recipient of a kidney, donated by her brother, David Clark—one of the earliest successful transplants. Mom and David even made the news. We were very hopeful.

But after about five years, the donated organ gave up the ghost. Eventually she qualified for a second transplant. But as Mom was being prepped in the operating room—doctors had actually opened her up and were prepared to begin the transplant—they discovered that the replacement kidney was damaged. Incredibly, due to some miscommunication, it had begun to decompose. The operation was called off. Mom had to recover without a new kidney. But she never could get healthy enough after that disaster to get back on the waiting list.

My mother was a straight-up warrior. But her chronic disease and long slide into infirmity, coupled with our inability to arrest it, to give her relief, to *rescue* her—all that cast a shadow over our childhoods. I dealt with it by getting out. From early boyhood, I felt a strong pull to be outdoors, and not just because we lived in a beautiful part of the world: the Oquirrh Mountains to the northwest and the Wasatch Range rising dramatically to the northeast, so stunning with the morning sun filtering through that those purple mountains might as well have been conjured by a CGI specialist.

The outdoors gave me a refuge, an escape from the heaviness of our home life. I would take our dog Rambo and

THE DANCE WITH DANGER

camp alone in the nearby canyons. When I got older, I'd head south with friends for spring break to play in the San Rafael Swell, mountain biking, hiking, canyoneering, and free-climbing (no ropes.)

I found release and relief in the outdoors. I never looked for that escape in beer or whiskey or weed. Yes, I abide by the rules of our church forbidding recreational drugs and alcohol. But I'm not really tempted to smoke or drink, so it doesn't feel like much of a sacrifice. I'm not looking to blunt reality; I'm trying to see it more clearly.

Which is not to say I adhered strictly to the law in my younger days. Starting around the time I was eleven, if no one else was home, I might grab the car keys and drive our family's Volkswagen hatchback through the neighborhood. I never invited any friends to ride shotgun. That would have been irresponsible.

There's always been a magnet in me drawing me toward danger. I like adrenaline, and I am drawn to people who like adrenaline. Such as my wife. But I'm getting ahead of myself.

On a class trip to Moab when I was in high school, a group of us hiked up to the Gemini Bridges, a pair of two-hundred-foot-long side-by-side bridge-like arches caused by years and years of water and wind erosion that has worn a crack or gap between those spans ranging from six to ten feet—like the Moon Door in that high castle in *Game of Thrones*.

For as long as that aperture has existed, it has called out this challenge to foolhardy visitors: You can make it—no problem! With a running start, they plant and leap and soar across the hole in the rock, landing safely on the far side and wondering, after the adrenaline abates, *What the hell was I thinking?* Once in a great while, a brash, confident person makes a misstep—slips or misjudges the distance—and doesn't quite make it to the far side, instead plunging two hundred feet to the rocks below.

In my group, I was the first to take that leap. What can I say? I was sixteen; my prefrontal cortex was not fully formed. I liked the lure of danger, that feeling of living on the edge. That rush, that dance with danger, is like a drug in its own right. Back then, that kind of risk-taking behavior made me feel completely alive. These days, with teenagers of my own, it's out of the question. Dear reader, do not take that leap, I implore you. It's not worth it.

My friends and I were also partial, in our teens, to homemade incendiaries such as dry-ice bombs. Put a little dry ice in a Gatorade bottle, add water, twist the cap back on, and you have eight to ten seconds before that blows. It's like a DIY M-80. We never blew up mailboxes or damaged property. It was enough for us to detonate a bomb on a quiet street around 8 or 9 p.m., watch the porch lights go on across the neighborhood, and haul ass on our bikes before the cops arrived.

To mix things up, my buddies and I would find some empty parking lot or school playground, put on thick gloves, squirt a bunch of lighter fluid on some tennis balls, and then engage in—well, they were firefights, weren't they? It was an unwritten rule that you never aimed a flaming Dunlop at someone's head. Sometimes when one of those tennis balls would hit one of us, it would splash a little lighter fluid on our jeans or sweatshirts, and for a few seconds, we might technically be on fire. That's when I learned the expression "stop, drop, and roll."

Another time in my preteens, a friend and I gathered under the back deck of his house, where we put some gunpowder in one-half of those plastic containers that held either a large gumball or a mini–NFL helmet in the quarter machines that seemed to be at the entrance of every grocery store in the Salt Lake Valley. We would then squeeze some modeling airplane glue on top of it and apply a lit match. We both were standing over it, looking down, when it went *kaboom*. I lost my eyebrows and nose hairs that afternoon. It was not a good look or smell.

Years later, while taking a polygraph test to become a state ranger, I was informed by one of the officers administering the test that making a dry-ice bomb is a second-degree felony in Utah. "I did not know that," I replied. That was no excuse, but it was the truth, as they were able to ascertain in real time. I was hired despite my dodgy history with dry-ice munitions and other incendiaries.

Another refuge for me as an adolescent was music. After almost two years in Arizona, we'd moved back to Utah halfway through my seventh-grade year. Moving in the middle of the school year can be rough. But one of my classes in my new middle school made the transition a lot easier—I liked it that much.

English lit? Pre-algebra? Nope. I'm talking about the percussion class I enrolled in. For a young adolescent boy, banging on something in the middle of each day was highly therapeutic. As it happened, that class led me to the welcoming, wonderful David Fullmer, who taught me at Provo's Timpview High School, so named for Mount Timpanogos, the daunting and glacier-hewn 11,752-foot massif looming over it. Mr. Fullmer decided I had the makings of a good drummer. I had rhythm skills—I had the beat!—and I ascended through the ranks to what Mr. Fullmer called "Drum Leader." I drummed all four years in high school and gained drummer friends for life.

I don't play drums anymore, other than to tenderize meat or treat the steering wheel of my truck as a kind of tom-tom while I crank 1970s and '80s vintage rock. As it turns out everything gives off a frequency, and you can drum on almost any surface. I'm always looking for a good beat. I wasn't surprised to read in a recent issue of *Modern Drummer* magazine that, according to a study conducted in Sweden, drummers who can easily keep rhythm tend to have better problem-solving skills. That article also referred to a second study, conducted by an Oxford psychologist, that announced that drummers "typically have higher pain thresholds than non-drummers." Sounds about right.

It's traditional for high school students who are LDS to take an hour out of each day for a "seminary" period. Those classes, devoted to scripture and spirituality, typically take place in a building that's near the school but not part of it. Kids who aren't members of the church are welcome, but they aren't expected to be there and are free to take an accredited class during that time.

I had a really good seminary instructor named Damon Bolli, an ex-army soldier who was jacked—the guy looked like he spent half the day knocking out push-ups—and had a knack for making the lessons of the gospel accessible and helping us apply them in our daily lives.

Thanks in part to him, in my police work and life in general, I look hard to see the best in people. If they're having an off day—whether leaning on their horn in the Walmart Supercenter parking lot or climbing in the backcountry—I'll make a conscious effort to see the person behind the incorrect action. Just because I'm in a position of authority does not mean I have to act all, you know, *authoritative*, like Bill Belichick or the Borg in *Star Trek*. I want to be approachable. I want people to trust the person behind the badge.

I practice what I like to describe as "optimistic policing." Are people going to break the law and then lie to us? Why, yes, they are—quite frequently! Even as I'm citing or arresting them, however, I am trying to look past their misdeeds and malfeasance to see their potential and not reduce them to just their actions in that moment. Damon, the ex-military spiritual sage, helped me see the world that way.

Another value Damon imparted was humility, a tool I found useful to keep my ego in check after beating him in an Eskimo stick pull in front of the entire seminary class. It's a contest of strength and balance where you try to pull your opponent off the ground using a broomstick and leverage.

While I did not go to college right out of high school, a few of my band friends enrolled at Brigham Young University (BYU), which has its main campus in Provo. They encouraged me to try out for drumline in the Cougar Marching Band that fall. To my surprise, I made the cut—despite not being enrolled as a student. To play, the leaders told me, I would have to take a class. I enrolled in a religion class based on the New Testament with a little money in my pocket, and BYU paid for it.

I spent that fall playing snare drum at Cougar football games. The team had a strong season, winning ten games—including a shock-the-world upset of Notre Dame in South Bend, Indiana. My band friends and I also got to rock out at the Copper Bowl in Tucson, where our guys rolled Oklahoma 31–6.

At that point, I was ready for the next season in my life. Completing a two-year mission is often described as a rite of passage for a young Latter-day Saint. As a nineteen-year-old in 1995, I was ready to embark on that quest. The church had over four hundred missions headquartered around the world. I personally was down to do some proselytizing in a warm-weather climate—Jamaica, perhaps, or Tahiti. Instead, the church sent me to Missouri.

"He Usually Hurt the Other Guy"

DETECTIVE: What about his skill with a firearm; did he shoot a lot?

LANCE'S MOTHER: He did. He loved to go practice.

DET.: Where did he shoot at?

LM: Up in the hills.

DET.: Did he go through a lot of ammo?

LM: Some days he did; some days he wouldn't.

DET.: How about the rifle? Was he good with the rifle?

LM: Yeah, I think so. He didn't practice as much [with the rifle]. He wanted to be more skilled with the handguns.

DET.: Did he hunt?

LM: No. He doesn't like the sight of blood. And he doesn't like killing animals.

DET.: [So he's] not a violent person, then? He ever been in any fights?

LM: Oh yeah, he loved to . . .

DET.: Liked to fight? How's that not a violent person? [*Laughs*]

LM: A violent person to me is someone that just goes and picks a fight.

DET.: So, um, where was he fighting at? Did he hang out in bars?

LM: Mostly just parties, out in the country.

DET.: Did he ever get hurt?

LM: No, he usually hurt the other guy.

. . .

DET.: Has he ever been violent toward you?

LM: Verbally.

DET.: Where's his father at?

LM: Salt Lake.

DET.: Did his father abuse him?

LM: No. It was his stepdad.

DET.: Was it physical or mental?

LM: Both.

DET.: Sexual abuse?

LM: No, physical.

DET.: How old was Lance when this was occurring?

LM: Started when he was thirteen.

Chapter 2

RUN AT THE FEAR

The proper name for my assignment was the Missouri Independence Mission, though that proved to be a bit of a misnomer. I actually spent more time in Kansas.

Most full-time Latter-day Saint missionaries are single young men and women in their late teens and early twenties. It's also a popular option for empty-nesting older couples who no longer have kids at home.

Then as now, the primary purpose of our mission was to help convert new members to the church by sharing the gospel of Jesus Christ. We would attach our black name tags to our starched-white shirts and go knocking on doors, passing out pamphlets and copies of the Bible and the Book of Mormon. More recently, church leaders have acknowledged that door-to-door proselytizing isn't the most efficient way to find new Latter-day Saints.

We also had other forms of outreach. When we asked people if they needed help—if there was anything we could do for them—we meant it literally. Unconditional, no-strings-attached service was, and remains, an important element of every mission. That's how we end up weeding, raking leaves, cleaning garages, helping folks move, volunteering at soup kitchens, and working with the unhoused or addicts. Maybe, during our interaction, we would make an impression or get someone to reflect on how they were living their lives. Perhaps we planted a seed.

My mission was a great adventure and also the hardest thing I'd ever done up to that point in my life—the opposite of a vacation. We had strict schedules and curfews. To keep our focus on the mission, we were instructed to avoid "worldly entertainment," such as TV or movies. We were allowed to call home twice a year: on Christmas and Mother's Day. (Today's missionaries are permitted weekly calls to family back home.)

We dealt with a lot of rejection, not all of it polite. But the experience was also deeply fulfilling and transformative. And surprising.

I can't remember who told us we absolutely *had* to dine at Gates BBQ in Kansas City, Missouri. But whoever it was, that person had an excellent sense of humor, as I was about to learn.

Founded in 1946, Gates occupies a prominent place in the pantheon of legendary barbecue joints, and rightfully so. Just thinking about those sandwiches makes my mouth water. One evening, following an afternoon of door-knocking, we decided to give Gates a try. Almost immediately, we were accosted. At least that's what it felt like.

An unsmiling woman behind the counter shouted at us, "How can I help you?" We looked at each other. Was she talking to us? There were ten or so people in line in front of us. Surely she wasn't talking to us. Then why was she now looking—no, *glaring*—at us? Then she repeated the question, this time with more edge and impatience: "How can I *help* you?" One of us tried explaining to her that this was our first time at Gates, and we needed another minute. She just rolled her eyes and asked the people behind us if she could help them.

Unlike us Latter-day Saints, all the other patrons seemed to have a firm command of the shorthand one needed to order at this joint:

"Beef and a half, please."

"Mixed plate beef, lean-as, fries well done, please."

"Combo and a half to go, please."

With assistance from some Good Samaritans in line around us, we got our orders in. When my sandwich came up, it took me about 1.5 seconds to realize that this food, those smoked meats slathered with that thick, sweet sauce—a sublime blend of brown sugar, molasses, and tomatoes—made the excruciating process of ordering it completely worthwhile.

As other customers filed in and got the same treatment, we realized that it wasn't about us. They were impolite-bordering-on-hostile to everyone! As it was later explained to me, that's their shtick. The metamessage is, *We're going to be rude to you, and you'll still come back—that's how good this barbecue is!*

And we did come back. The process of ordering was far less painful once we figured out what we wanted and how to ask for it.

Dining at Gates, I realized in retrospect, was kind of a microcosm of my mission: It was daunting in the beginning, and it was uncomfortable, and we dealt with some rude people, it's true. But the payoff was amazing.

At the time I was assigned to the Missouri Independence Mission, I didn't know much about the Show Me State, other than that it was in the middle of the country and that it was the starting point for the Lewis and Clark expedition. I'd only heard stories—and would hear more upon arriving at the mission—of how western Missouri played an oversized role in the early history of our church.

After visiting Independence, Missouri, in the summer of 1831, church founder Joseph Smith surprised his followers by announcing that this frontier hamlet had been the site of the Garden of Eden from the Old Testament. Independence and its environs, he declared, would become the "center place" of Zion—a declaration that gave rise to a steady migration of Latter-day Saints to western Missouri, all eager to reside on such sacred ground.

That influx alarmed the settlers who already lived there and led to a series of conflicts and forced relocations that culminated in 1838, when Governor Lilburn Boggs, accusing Latter-day Saints of defying the law and making war on the citizens of Missouri, issued an executive order calling for Mormons to be "exterminated or driven from the State if necessary."

Upon receiving that order, General Samuel D. Lucas marched on the Mormon stronghold of the Far West.

Latter-day Saints were forced to surrender their arms and, at bayonet point, sign deeds that gave their property to the state of Missouri. All Saints were ordered to be out of the state by spring.

That action led to a mass migration of up to fifteen thousand church members to neighboring Illinois and Iowa. Harassed and robbed by vigilantes and exposed to the elements, many suffered greatly during this forced exodus, and some died.

As decades passed, more and more Missourians came to recognize the immorality of that state-sponsored violence against a religious minority. In 1976, then Missouri governor Kit Bond signed an executive order officially rescinding Boggs's extermination order, declaring that it "clearly contravened the rights to life, liberty, property and religious freedom" by the constitutions of the United States and the state of Missouri. Bond expressed "deep regret for the injustice and undue suffering" the order had caused the Latter-day Saints.

Thirty-four years later, addressing a group of Saints in 2010, Bond remained incredulous at the treatment of Mormon people in 1830s Missouri, describing it as "beyond barbaric." "We cannot change history," he went on, "but we certainly ought to be able to learn from it and, where possible, acknowledge past mistakes."

I learned much of that history in the years that followed. At the time, I was a wide-eyed teenager who'd never left home. I had a lot of anxiety about moving to the Midwest. I'd never had a brother, but I would be assigned a "companion"—and do very little throughout the day when not in the presence of that person. That enforced familiarity—not quite having a conjoined twin but not so far from it either—would require a lot of give and take, as in any relationship. How would that go?

This isn't a book about religion, so I'll boil this down to the basics: when we're sharing the gospel, our message to people is that they're not alone, that Jesus is there for them and wants what's best for them. It was one thing to know that message and try to live it. It was quite another to knock on the doors of strangers and then try to talk them into opening their hearts to it. That was a long, long way from my comfort zone. I was excited and scared at the same time. And it was on this mission that I learned how to "run at the fear"—a motto and mantra I've found helpful to live by.

Instead of worrying about the unknowns, I embraced them—turned them into knowns. Ernest Hemingway once wrote that "the shortest answer is doing the thing," which I've chosen to interpret as a call to action. Don't sit there dithering, agonizing, hand-wringing like Hamlet. Consider your options, weigh the consequences, make a decision. Tear off the Band-Aid. Ask the uncomfortable question. Deliver the news, good or bad. Ring the doorbell. You might find yourself looking at a person whose heart is open to your message.

You never know when those words might serve as water to the spiritually parched. It doesn't happen often, which is why it's so cool and memorable when it does. Seeing someone commit to change their life at such a profound level—it's an amazing thing to be a part of.

When it comes to conversion of our faith in Jesus Christ, some parts of the world are much more difficult than others. Missionaries in South America might baptize hundreds of converts. For a variety of reasons, it's far more difficult for us to get traction in Scandinavian countries and Europe. For example, my brother-in-law spent two years in Germany and got shut out. Zero converts. In Kansas and Missouri, I fell between those two extremes, probably averaging about one baptism per month, although I hesitate to share even that rough estimate, because I don't mean to imply that it's a numbers game.

Just as I figured out after that first excruciating visit how to order at Gates BBQ, I got past the anxiety I'd felt around asking strangers for a moment of their time. That doesn't mean I didn't get a bunch of doors closed in my face. I just learned not to take it personally.

The people we meet in this life tend to fall into two categories: they can be a blessing or a lesson. And we learn from both, right? As it turns out, one of the most effective influences in my life turned out to be the man who tried to end it.

"He Shoved My Head into the Window"

The following is an excerpt from a 2024 interview with Sandee Arellano, Lance's ex-wife:

SANDEE ARELLANO: We started dating when I was sixteen or seventeen. His parents were divorced, he was kind of a pothead. We were kind of stoners back in the day, unfortunately. He had transferred over to Bingham [High School, in South Jordan, Utah,] my junior year, I think. He was only there a year or two. A lot of the things he really liked to do was Jeep and camp and fish.

INTERVIEWER: Could he be kind and sweet? What was it that drew you to him?

SA: I don't even know if I can put a pinpoint on that. I think a lot of it with me was, I'm the type that thinks, "I'm gonna fix ya." I was the one always bringing home [stray] cats, and I started bringing home people I guess. [*Laughs*] My parents were the same way. I had just lost my brother the same year I met Lance. And I think in some way my parents thought maybe this is our second chance with this one.

I: I'm sorry about your brother. What happened to him?

SA: He was on his way to work and had to change his tire on the freeway and somebody hit him. . . . [Lance] was a drug dealer in high school. My parents had to pay off his drug debt. He owed his dealer, and they were coming after him. And here's the family that wants to frickin' fix everybody.

I: What do you remember of your wedding day?

SA: Oh God, my wedding. That right there should've been [a bright-red flag], like, What the hell are you thinking? It was in South Jordan. The ceremony was great. My parents paid for it, it was gorgeous, everything was beautiful. We went there in the morning to do the rehearsal stuff. [An Arellano family member] said, "Hey, you're not supposed to see the bride till you get married." So Lance is like, "I'll see you at the wedding." And then, when he got there, I could smell the alcohol on his breath, and I was like, "Oh, you've been drinking all day? This is gonna be great fun." We had a champagne fountain [at the reception], and my dad had ordered a full bar, because all his friends were coming. We left, and we were supposed to have an after-party at [Lance's] dad's. Well, he decides it's time to have a fistfight in the front yard with his dad. Instead of them dealing with him, [a member of Lance's family] said, "You need to get him in the car and take him home." He hit my head on the windshield that night. That was my wedding night.

I: You were inside or outside the car when that happened?

SA: I was inside the car. He shoved my head into the window. I kicked him out of the apartment, and I didn't see him for about a month. I should have just kept on going. But I was the one [thinking], "Oh I can handle this. I'm gonna make this right."

Chapter 3

"THE COURSE OF TRUE LOVE NEVER DID RUN SMOOTH"

My time in the Midwest changed me in important, positive ways. The rigorous schedule, the forced abstention from simple entertainment—TV shows, movies, my beloved classic rock—made me stronger, more disciplined. I learned that I can do hard things. The emphasis on service, on helping others, made me more selfless. Usually. Often. Sometimes.

Sharing with people the core beliefs of our church and answering questions about it resulted in a kind of enforced reflection that deepened my own faith—and, incidentally, gave me added confidence in my speaking skills.

Now back in Provo after my mission, how would I harness this newfound strength and selflessness and confidence? I became a used car salesman. That's right, I went from selling Jesus to selling jalopies. Hey, man—I needed a job!

I'd moved back in with my parents, who were delighted to have me back but also marveled at the volume of groceries I could go through. I needed to pitch in financially—I needed to pull my own weight. One of my sisters knew a guy who ran a used car lot south of Provo. I dropped by the lot and offered my services. He asked me if I had any sales experience. I told him I'd just returned from a two-year mission. Got hired on the spot.

It was a long summer that left me wondering how certain attorneys and lobbyists can live with themselves. Sometimes, our customers got solid deals. And other times, they put down cash for lemons. I never sold a car that I knew had specific problems without disclosing them first. But there were still a lot of times when issues arose—a carburetor went on the fritz, a transmission gave up the ghost—not long after people drove off the lot. Those customers called back, rightfully upset. And we had to break the bad news: they'd bought the vehicle "as is," so it was their problem now.

I'm a pleaser. I want people to like me. Being the villain in someone's life was diametrically opposed to my conception of myself. It bothered me. One of the happiest days of my life was walking off that lot for the last time at the end of the summer.

I enrolled that fall as a student at Utah Valley University. There, I shared with my newfound friend Don Vandyke the stressful saga of my summer peddling used cars. After commiserating with me, Don told me about a newly created High Adventure camp in Moab, featuring hiking, rock climbing, and river rafting. Don had signed on to work there the following summer and told me he'd be happy to recommend me to his bosses. This involved hosting fourteen- to eighteen-year-olds for a few days at a time, guiding them through mountain biking, rappelling from cliffs with a rope and harness, and river rafting. He had no way of knowing that he was changing the course of my life.

For folks who haven't visited this corner of Utah or know it only as a mountain biking mecca, here are a few pages on its history. Certain prophetic books of the Bible make frequent mention of Moab, a kingdom on the eastern shore of the Dead Sea. The Utah version of Moab, the seat of sparsely populated Grand County, is cupped in a bend of the Colorado, the name of both the river and the state whose Rocky Mountain National Forest forms its headwaters, four hundred miles to the north and east.

Moab sits in the heart of the Canyonlands section of the Colorado Plateau, an area of high desert covering 130,000 square miles, pushed up thousands of feet by hot mantle rock beneath it. The Colorado Plateau is centered (almost) on the Four Corners region of the American Southwest and is named for the same river that, over six million years, carved the Grand Canyon.

It's a part of the world that wears its geology on its sleeve, a region renowned for its exposed bedrock, much of it rich in iron, which, upon exposure to oxygen, becomes iron oxide, turning that rock into some shade of red: vermilion, pink, and ocher—a natural clay pigment composed of the mineral hematite, a word whose root derives from the Greek word for blood.

According to an exhibit at the Moab Museum, for some ten thousand years before the arrival of European explorers, countless tribes wandered over the plateau, "developing a complex relationship with its ecosystem, their roles within it, and in turn, adopting cultural traditions and ceremonies based on learned respect for the land and its resources." The tribes whose relationships to the land have been shared through written word and oral histories are the ones with whom we're most familiar—the Ute, Navajo, Paiute, and Hopi.

Moab offered a convenient crossing of the Colorado for traders and settlers traversing the Old Spanish Trail, which linked Santa Fe and Los Angeles. In 1855, some forty men left Salt Lake City with instructions to establish a mission in the area now known as Moab. After two months of laborious travel, accompanied by seventy-five head of cattle, those redoubtable Saints forded the Grand River (it wasn't renamed the Colorado until 1921), then set about constructing a modest stone fort—whose walls, historians note, went up mere feet from the site of the city's Motel 6.

Amicable at first, their relations with the Ute Indian tribe—whose lands they sought to annex—deteriorated swiftly, culminating in a series of gun battles that left three missionaries and several Utes dead. The Indians then burned the settlers' crops. The missionaries abandoned the fort the next day, leaving five horses and most of their cattle behind. It would be two decades before any white settlers ventured back to establish a permanent settlement in that valley.

The following is a brief list of Moab milestones, not all of them cheerful. In 1883, the Denver and Rio Grande Western Railroad opted to bypass the town, instead laying tracks through Thompson Springs and Cisco to the north. A camp outside Moab was used as a citizen isolation center to incarcerate "troublemaking" Japanese American citizens unjustly interned during World War II. And in 1952, a plucky geologist named Charles Steen discovered a rich deposit of high-grade uranium thirty miles south of town. Steen's strike coincided with the US government's concerted push, at the dawn of the Cold War, to secure a domestic supply of uranium capable of sustaining its nuclear weapons program.

Months after living with his wife and their four boys in a tarpaper shack, Steen was suddenly a millionaire and, for $250,000, built a hilltop mansion, complete with a greenhouse, servants' quarters, and the largest swimming pool in the state.

A generous man, he donated property to local schools and built "Steenville," a housing development for his employees, to whom he extended low-interest mortgage loans. The opposite of thrifty, Steen was known for treating himself to a new red Lincoln Continental every year.

Moab became known as the "Uranium Capital of the World"—a title that lasted about as long as Steen's fortune. Having sated its need for uranium, the US government stopped subsidizing high prices for it, kneecapping the market.

Steen filed for bankruptcy, and his assets were seized by the IRS. He died in 2006, and his mansion is now the site of the Sunset Grill, the oldest operating restaurant in Moab.

In recent decades, the city has enjoyed a renaissance as a mecca for outdoor enthusiasts of varying stripes, from hikers,

NINE MIRACLES

mountain bikers, and river rafters to Jeepers, rock climbers, and BASE jumpers. With its nearby national parks, countless trails, and, of course, the Colorado, Moab now serves as a springboard for countless adrenaline-intensive adventures.

Not all those thrill seekers exercise good judgment, however, which keeps the rangers in those parks—along with Moab's EMTs, paramedics, and occasionally the county coroner—quite busy. When the subject arose of city mottos and slogans, such as "Cleveland Rocks" and "What Happens in Vegas, Stays in Vegas," a paramedic friend of mine suggested this one for our town: "Moab—Your Final Destination."

In the summer of 1998, thanks to Don Vandyke, I drove down to start my job with the High Adventure camp. It was going to be fun getting young people out into the backcountry, and I was looking forward to having a few adventures myself.

One morning in late June, our camp had scheduled a rafting trip for some Boy Scouts we were hosting. But the company we contracted with was short a river guide. No big deal: they called Western River Expeditions, which rented them a guide for the day. That guide was one Wendy Elggren, an eyelash shy of six feet tall, with corn-silk blonde hair and better muscle tone than most of the teenaged scouts she would be leading down the river that day. An ex–high school swimmer from Sandy, Utah, she would go on to row for the crew team at the University of Utah.

As Wendy stepped off the bus and walked down to the water at the Hittle Bottom campground, where we launched

"THE COURSE OF TRUE LOVE NEVER DID RUN SMOOTH"

the rafts that morning, she had my full attention. She was pleasant and quick to smile, but we all learned early on there was iron beneath her good cheer. Wendy took zero guff from any of us and gave as good as she got in water fights. A few of the bolder scouts tried to bump her off the raft. Invariably, they failed and ended up in the drink themselves.

I tried drawing her out, but she wasn't giving me much:

"Where you from?"

"Sandy."

"Brothers and sisters?"

"Three sisters."

"I have three sisters too!"

She found that coincidence far less remarkable than I did.

I didn't mean to stare, but Wendy did have some odd tan lines. Her arms were bronze below the shoulder and quite pale above. Her legs were white down to just below her knees, and her suntanned shins contrasted sharply with her pale feet. When I congratulated her on her advanced farmer's tan, she didn't laugh but instead gave me another fierce look and replied, "I got back from my mission three days ago." She'd spent eighteen months in Indiana. It was cold and flat, she recalled when I asked about it. "But the people were fun."

I told her a little about my time in Kansas and Missouri. But mostly, I asked her questions about being a river guide. While I would later start closing the gap, Wendy was much more comfortable on the water than I. She'd already guided a full season for Western River Expeditions before heading to Indiana. It was fun to see her skills on display—her strength and finesse and ability to read the water as if it was the top row on an optometrist's eye chart.

I was quite taken with Wendy and only a little discouraged afterward when I asked for her phone number and she said no.

"Really? Why?" I asked.

"I don't know what my number is," she explained. "I just moved here yesterday."

"How about if I drop by and see you sometime?" I suggested. "Would that be cool?"

"That would be OK," she assented.

Now we were getting somewhere! "What's your address?" I asked.

"I don't know. I just moved in," she said, then adding as a consolation, "I'm sure we'll see each other around."

These were minor setbacks, as was the report I received from a friend later that night that he'd seen her on the back of some guy's motorcycle. I wasn't that dismayed. As Lysander says in *A Midsummer Night's Dream*, "The course of true love never did run smooth." (A river metaphor in Shakespeare!) I was playing the long game. I had all summer.

Not too long ago, I listened in as Wendy described the halting, early nature of our unconventional courtship: "He found me eventually. He got my phone number from someone else. That's how we ended up dating. We went out a bit. I didn't ever date one guy exclusively. I dated lots of people

"THE COURSE OF TRUE LOVE NEVER DID RUN SMOOTH"

while I was dating him." (Just for the record, I wasn't dating anyone else when I was seeing Wendy.) She continued, "My mission president told me I had to date people when I came home from my mission. But I was in no hurry whatsoever to get married. I was happy working on the river."

The more we talked, the better I understood her and her deep connection to the Colorado River. Wendy has a sister 368 days older than she is. Shelley was homecoming queen and student body president. While whip-smart herself, Wendy definitely did not gravitate toward tiaras and homecoming courts and getting her picture in the yearbook. She was painfully shy. It didn't help that people often pointed out the marked contrast between the outgoing, overachieving older sister and her more reserved younger sister.

Just after Wendy graduated from high school, their family took a trip to Moab and signed up for the expedition that changed her life. It was just a day trip, she recalls: "I hopped on the boat, and just immediately, I was like, 'Oh, I want to do *this*.'" She watched how the guide used the raft's oars to propel and steer it. After studying the boatman's techniques for a while, Wendy asked if she could give it a try. She ended up rowing the entire day. When flatwater gave way to whitewater, the guide talked her through it and taught her to look—and think—ahead, to read the river, and how and where to position the boat. Turned out, Wendy was a natural.

When she told her parents afterward that she had found her purpose, they smiled at her, confident that this infatuation would pass. It did not. All through her first semester at the University of Utah, she heard the call of the river.

Wendy applied that December to be a guide at Western River Expeditions and was crushed when she wasn't chosen. She was passed over, the manager later explained, because she was so quiet. Management didn't think she could be assertive enough to do the job. But one of the bosses called Wendy that April and threw her a lifeline. Each spring, the company holds a three-week training course for new hires. This year, the man explained, they'd decided to invite two "alternates" to participate. The alternates would not be paid for the training, he emphasized, and were not guaranteed a job. Wendy accepted on the spot, even though it meant she would miss three weeks of classes. "I'm still not sure how I passed my finals," she says.

There were a series of clinics and competitions to see who could finish an obstacle course the fastest, who could pitch a tent the fastest, who could set up the groover fastest. (The groover is a portable toilet, a box with some chemicals in the bottom and a toilet seat attached—the first thing set up in a camp and the last to be taken down.) In the end, the universe provided. The company parted ways with a pair of guides, making space for Wendy and a friend. She was in.

One of Western River Expeditions' popular day trips is Westwater Canyon, a seventeen-mile stretch whose calm start and serene finish bookend an adrenaline-intensive whitewater section including such advanced rapids as

"THE COURSE OF TRUE LOVE NEVER DID RUN SMOOTH"

Funnel Falls, Skull Rapid, and Sock-It-to-Me Rapids. The company rarely allowed first-year guides to row clients down that section. But Wendy was an exception, guiding that trip nineteen times her first season. She rowed big water that entire summer.

She blossomed in other ways too. It was a season of self-discovery. To illustrate just how bashful and introverted Wendy had been as an adolescent, her mother, Debbie, tells the story of how Wendy would call the number for takeout pizza, then hand the phone to her sister Stephanie rather than endure the ordeal of speaking to a stranger. But with her people, on the river, Wendy found a wellspring of confidence. "This was my spot, these were my friends, and it had nothing to do with my sister or anything else," she confided in me. "I had been waiting twenty years to find that girl."

In addition to providing her with an identity, the river put her in the proximity of various suitors, including me. While I wasn't the only guy she was dating, I believe I was the leader in the clubhouse. After that first river season ended in 1998, Wendy and I both headed back north for another year of college. We kept dating.

When she told me she was headed back to Moab the following summer, I applied to be a guide at Western River. I thought it would be helpful, while I was interviewing for that job, to casually mention that I was seeing Wendy Elggren. Unbeknownst to me, another guy she'd been dating, who was also in the running for a guiding job, let it drop that *he* was Wendy's boyfriend.

"Neither of them is my boyfriend," she told her boss when he asked her about it. "They're just . . . boys I do stuff with."

"Well," he asked, after digesting that reply, "which one should I hire?"

"That's your job," she said. "You're the boss."

I took it as a challenge rather than a defeat when she inserted distance between us. "I kept trying to break up with him," she told a reporter in 2023. "But then something would happen, like, his mom would have a stroke."

While Wendy may not have been certain I was "the one," her parents were in my corner. They would invite me to family functions Wendy was expected to attend. She would show up, and—surprise!—I'd be there.

Some women in our church speak of a pervasive pressure—a shared, communal expectation, sometimes subtle, sometimes not—to marry, raise children, and be a "helpmeet" to their husbands. Fiercely independent as she was (and is), Wendy sometimes chafed at those assumptions. She wasn't pushing *me* away, I like to think, so much as she was buying herself some time. Her top priorities back then were earning her degree at the University of Utah and running the Colorado River, which thrilled her and filled her up.

In the winter of 1998, after my first summer seeing her, I started steering our conversations toward the *M* word. Gracefully, tactfully—but pointedly—she would change the subject.

Then came what I can only describe as a custodial epiphany. At the end of the river season, Wendy returned to

"THE COURSE OF TRUE LOVE NEVER DID RUN SMOOTH"

college, where she had declared a half dozen majors through the years but ended up earning her degree in sanitation, nutrition, and diseases in developing countries. She ended up earning enough credits to graduate twice—minus a single class. Wendy is the opposite of incurious.

To pay for all those classes, she landed a gig that was unglamorous but well paying. She was a janitor, cleaning bathrooms at night at a high-rise in Salt Lake City. She liked the job because it didn't require her to talk to people. She could just lock the door, put on her headphones, and rock out while she worked.

One night—she swears this happened—she heard a voice say, "You should marry Brody."

That's weird, she thought. *I just locked everyone out. No one is in this bathroom with me.* She checked the door—still locked—and went back to work. She heard the voice again: "You should marry Brody." When Wendy tells the story—always to big laughs—those instructions emanate from one of the toilets.

Wher*ever* that voice came from, I'm grateful for the assist. That said, I'd like to believe that if some divine guidance was issued that night, it came from an air vent, or paper towel dispenser, or sprinkler. Anything but a commode.

Less than a month later, we went up to Deer Creek Reservoir for kayaking and a picnic, and I proposed. She said yes. (Thanks, mysterious lavatory voice!) Then we went back to the car. Both of us were freezing. It was unseasonably cold.

From our courtship to Wendy's revelation in the men's room to her sometimes rocky dealings with some members of my family, our relationship is untraditional. It doesn't conform to notions of how people react and behave when they're in love.

That's partly because Wendy is the most authentic person I know. She's not prickly per se so much as she simply has no bandwidth for BS or superficiality. Fit, strong, and beautiful though she may be, she's not that concerned about her appearance or wardrobe. If our house doesn't look like it's just been staged for a *Dwell* magazine photo shoot, she's not losing sleep over it. None of us are.

Not only am I not put off by her strength and independence and inclination to go against the grain; it's what drew me to her in the first place.

What drew her to *me*? Shared values, shared faith, a deep comfort level with each other, and a shared abiding passion for running the Colorado River.

Although I would debate the point, Wendy had guys pursuing her who might have been considered more *conventionally* handsome than I. But I was steadfast, reliable, constant. I just kept coming back, and in the end, I wore her down until she knew in her bones that I was her best bet for the long haul. The talking toilet just sealed the deal.

In that Shakespeare play I mentioned, *A Midsummer Night's Dream*, Lysander is in love with Hermia, who loves him in return but has been ordered by her father, Theseus, to marry a different guy. She rebels against Theseus, who

"THE COURSE OF TRUE LOVE NEVER DID RUN SMOOTH"

is described by the Harvard scholar Marjorie Garber as "a strong central figure of authority who attempts to order the world." But Hermia would not be ordered. Nor would Wendy Elggren. Wise for his years, Lysander is wary of the fleeting, flash-bang nature of young love—that it can be

> Swift as a shadow, short as any dream,
> Brief as the lightning . . .
> So quick bright things come to confusion.

Lasting relationships, the ones with legs, are sustained by more than that early ardor—that lightning. They're built on a foundation of trust, mutual sacrifice, and compromise. And laughter. While it might look slightly unusual from the outside, our marriage was built on that bedrock. That was going to help a lot in the rough waters ahead.

"He Always Had That Explosive Anger"

The following is an excerpt from a 2024 interview with Sandee Arellano, Lance's ex-wife:

SANDEE ARELLANO: The sad thing was, he terrified me so much, I didn't feel safe with a cop. That's why I never called the cops. I was worried what he was going to do [if they didn't take him in].

We had a really bad fight in our first apartment [in Midvale, Utah]. The upstairs people called the cops. I had left the situation, and the police said, "You want to come back and meet us at your apartment?" and I was like, "You can have my key, but I'm not going in with you."

And all the sudden you see them hauling him out, because he's decided to take on all three of them.

He always had that explosive anger. He could be the sweetest person, then all the sudden be the most ruthless person.

It wasn't a healthy relationship. It just took me getting old enough and mature enough to say, "OK, we'd had our ride. Time to let go."

Chapter 4

FROM RIVER GUIDE TO RANGER

Like geese and some circus performers, Wendy and I followed a seasonal migration pattern: college and work in Salt Lake City in fall, winter, and most of the spring and then south to Moab for the river season.

It only took one summer of river guiding for that lifestyle to get into my bloodstream. I returned to Western River Expeditions for the next five seasons. While both of us loved the job, Wendy and I piloted different boats. She only had eyes for her beloved oar rigs, steering and maneuvering the raft through the rapids with deft strokes of those oars.

I became a "motorhead," leading trips in sturdy craft called J rigs and S rigs, which plied the river with help from an outboard four-stroke motor. Fully loaded with food, gear, and clients, they could weigh five and a half tons. They were fun, very stable, and—I appreciated this—almost impossible to flip.

Back in Salt Lake in the colder months, we worked various jobs. For a couple years, we managed apartments for my uncle Bob, who is a great guy (for a landlord) with a unique sense of style: he favors ostrich-skin boots and gold chains—fashion choices not often made by men in the

Church of Jesus Christ of Latter-day Saints—but gives of his time serving others.

Bob let us live rent-free in the complex we managed, a sweet deal. When river season arrived, we'd sublet the place to friends who could manage the units for us, then head down to Moab.

When she wasn't on the water, Wendy had a side hustle as a skip tracer—a kind of private investigator who researches public records, social media, and other databases to locate a person who's gone missing. Her dad is an attorney who owns a collection firm. Wendy's been helping him locate missing persons (and their assets) since she was a teenager. She enjoys the work and is relentless as a Ringwraith in J. R. R. Tolkien's Middle-earth. I wouldn't sleep well knowing she was looking for me.

But every January, Wendy would come down with a raging case of "River Fever" and start talking about snowpack in the Rockies, predicting when the Colorado might awaken from its hibernation and start cranking.

As much as we both craved the challenge and adventure—and, yes, the danger—of that river, we looked forward just as much to reuniting with our fellow guides, who'd become some of our closest friends. Which makes sense, if you think about it: working on the river—on multiday trips in particular—we saw one another in our best and worst moments. We helped one another through trying conditions that included very difficult stretches of rapids and, once in a while, very difficult clients.

FROM RIVER GUIDE TO RANGER

Wendy always got a little downcast when September came around and it was time to head north out of the Canyonlands and back to Salt Lake. Since the initial moments of her first visit to this valley in 1995, the place felt like home to her.

How much did Wendy love running the river? Well, she was thirty-four weeks pregnant with our first child, Stryder, and still taking customers through the rapids when the bosses took her aside and said maybe it was time to come off the water.

I graduated from the U in 2003 with a degree in psychology. (I was a single credit shy of double majoring in sociology but simply was not up for another semester.) Stryder was born the following year. We lived in a little fixer-upper in Riverton, twenty miles south of Salt Lake City. I'm OK admitting that Wendy did most of the fixing.

By then we'd fallen hard for Moab and were looking for ways to make it our permanent home. Exhilarating and fulfilling as we found it, river guiding wasn't a lifestyle conducive to raising a young family. It was also, as Wendy put it, "wicked hard on our bodies." So we put the word out to our Moab friends to send up a flare if they learned of any full-time job opportunities down there that would pay a modest mortgage and support a small family.

We are eternally grateful to our friend Janel Arbon, who thought of us when her husband, Jeff, decided to leave his job with the Utah Division of Parks and Recreation and become a state trooper. Jeff had been an off-highway/river ranger for Utah State Parks. His duties included boating patrols on the

Green, San Juan, and Colorado Rivers. He also worked the backcountry, enforcing laws and assisting hikers and bikers in distress. With Jeff moving over to the Utah Highway Patrol, Utah State Parks would be looking to replace him. Janel gave us the heads-up, and I applied for that job.

Utah State Parks has plenty of rangers capable of operating boats on lakes and reservoirs. "But when it came to river dynamics—moving current, whitewater—we didn't have that expertise," noted Tony White, the regional lieutenant who interviewed me for that job. The ideal candidate would have river-guiding skills but the temperament of a law enforcement officer. The second half of that equation washed out a lot of applicants.

River guides are "kind of back to nature—they like their freedom," noted Lieutenant White. In addition to working on the water, this specialized agent would "go through formalized police training, deal with a lot of government bureaucracy and protocols, work crazy hours, and carry a firearm"—responsibilities that didn't overlap with their duties as river guides.

"Bringing all those things together made for a bit of a complicated candidate search," he told a reporter. "Brody was the one who brought it together—he had the river skills and was also someone who could wear a uniform on a daily basis and represent us in a professional manner. And he was just a nice guy."

While I have sometimes described my former river-guiding self as a "hippie" and for a year or so in my early twenties may have gone through an ill-advised afro phase, during that job interview, I qualified that, explaining that I was a *clean* hippie. I have long believed that ex-hippies make the best cops. We like people. And we're often familiar with the other side of the law.

Landing that job allowed us to move to Moab full time, which was easier said than done. Even then, the housing market was quite tight. We'd had realtors on the lookout for something in our price range for months and months, to no avail.

Meanwhile, we needed a place to stay. A rival rafting company, Worldwide River Expeditions, owned a trailer it used to lodge its guides. It was beyond generous of them to let us stay there, with baby Stryder in tow, until we found a place.

We arrived in Moab late on a Saturday. During our walk to church the next morning, we looked down the road and spied a "For Sale" sign in the distance with a phone number. We called it from the church phone, went to see the house after the meeting, and made an offer that afternoon—the first of seven the owner fielded that day.

Despite the competition, we got the house. It was the last house in the history of Moab, I am convinced, to sell for under $200,000. "You see?" said Wendy after the deal closed. "We're *meant* to be here!"

But was I meant to be a state ranger? Did I have the temperament for it? Gaining a small house for a small family was a huge relief. Now I could focus on mastering the skills of a

NINE MIRACLES

park ranger. When people think of park rangers, they might envision a pleasant, possibly earnest, and nature-loving person in a kiosk, collecting a fee, dispensing a map, recommending a trail or two, and then warning the visitors against rattlesnakes or poison oak. Hopefully they don't think—for very long, at least—of Alcatraz Island ranger John (Vicki) Johnson, played to deadpan perfection by the late Phil Hartman in *So I Married an Axe Murderer*.

But the fact is, Utah state park rangers are POST certified, meaning we've graduated from the Utah Peace Officer Standards and Training Academy. We're full-fledged law enforcement officers, trained in the law, patrol tactics, and, yes, firearms.

On my first day at the POST Academy, the instructors screened an unsettling video. The officer in the frame makes contact with a subject in a car, then seems oblivious, or paralyzed, as that subject reaches for a rifle, loads the magazine, arms the rifle, then kills him.

"This is especially for you guys," lectured an instructor, fixing his gaze on me and another park ranger. "You're out in the backcountry, isolated. You don't know *who* you're gonna run into out there. You've got to stay vigilant." That video made a deep impression on me. I'm a gregarious person, but from very early in my career as a ranger, I took my firearms training very seriously.

The Greek poet and mercenary soldier Archilochus was killed in battle at the age of thirty-five. Dude's been dead for 2,800 years, which makes his staying power all the more impressive. In addition to having a genus of hummingbird named after him, the warrior-poet has earned more recent renown for this astute observation: "We don't rise to the level of our expectations; we fall to the level of our training."

Olympic athletes don't line up for their events and hope they'll rise to the occasion. They expect to replicate, or slightly improve upon, efforts they've practiced a thousand times under similar pressure and duress. It's also why schools conduct fire drills. In moments of emergency, we default to our training. We do what we have practiced doing.

Alan Parrington, a former US Air Force fighter pilot and retired colonel, served in the 1990s as commander of that service's Academy Flying Training program. Some 80 percent of the cadets in that program were required to take "free-fall parachute training," Parrington recalled in 2017. This vexed bean counters in Congress, who asked why money was being spent teaching so many cadets a skill most of them would never use. Half the graduates would not end up flying, after all, and fewer than 5 percent would ever eject or bail out of a plane. So what was the point?

The point, Parrington wrote, came from the cadets themselves during their first two or three jumps: "They were so scared, they remembered nothing of the experience and only did what had been instinctively drilled into them during their training." That object lesson—you fall to the level of your training (in their case, literally)—taught them "to believe in their training, their leadership, their equipment, their service and themselves, which extended later into combat itself."

We fall to the level of our training: Lieutenant White understood this on a profound level. He checked in with me frequently during the sixteen-week training academy, making sure I had the equipment I needed and asking if I wanted to review any of the material with him or brush up on my skills. Until his retirement in January 2020, he was also my lead firearms instructor. We practiced together at our annual Ranger Academy. But we'd also head to the range sometimes on weekends, in our private time, to keep our skills sharp.

Why was it so imperative that I hone those skills? I'd been hired as a river ranger and spent a lot of my time on the boat ramp or on the water, talking to people in swimsuits and lifejackets, warning them to be careful of the currents in the river. Some days the biggest threat I faced was a middle schooler with a Super Soaker. My job entailed a lot of what Tim Smith, my supervisor, called "low-key law enforcement."

But I wasn't always on the water, especially in the offseason—autumn and winter. The job also took me into some remote parts of the backcountry. Yes, we work in state parks and on public land consisting of the Bureau of Land Management, School and Institutional Trust Lands, Sovereign Lands, and public waterways statewide. But that doesn't mean there aren't some dangerous people out there.

As White often reminded us, everyone likes a nature buzz. Bad guys spend time in parks too. The same criminal element that exists in a city or town—"those people recreate also," he would say. And then we'd go to work on what he called "disabled officer drills."

FROM RIVER GUIDE TO RANGER

For that exercise, we'd set up a scenario where the officer had been injured—sometimes by gunfire, sometimes by a car crash. Because I was left-handed, White would say, "You've been in a crash, your airbag's deployed, you've dislocated your left shoulder, and now you're taking gunfire. What do you do?" I would exit the vehicle, then cross draw my service weapon. That means I'd reach across my body with my right, nonshooting hand to unholster the gun and then return fire with that hand.

Regardless of which index finger was pulling the trigger, right or left, we'd been trained to count our rounds as we squeezed them off. All of us became proficient not just at shooting with our nondominant hand but also at reloading—stripping the spent magazine from the weapon, then inserting another, even if we had to hold the gun between our knees and do it one-handed. It would become clear, in the fullness of time, that White was doing more, during those drills on the range, than making me an ambidextrous marksman. He was helping save my life.

Even on weekends, even when we were on our own time, these sessions at the shooting range were not social visits. I mean, we chatted and caught up while signing in. But from my earliest exposure to White, I was struck by his level of seriousness when it came to training—to practicing and rehearsing these movements until we could perform them without really thinking, until they became muscle memory.

Did I say "muscle memory"? I stand corrected. Like many others in his field, the Australian neuroscientist Alan

Pearce prefers the term "motor memory." After all, movements we perform so often we can do them without conscious thought—riding a bike, throwing a baseball, tying our shoes—are the result of a motor learning process. "It is about the central nervous system, which is the brain and spinal cord, retaining motor skills and being able to memorize motor skills," Pearce recently told the Australian Broadcasting Corporation. That could apply to memorizing a tennis forehand or playing "Chopsticks" on the piano. Or in the case of peace officers under White's tutelage, shooting with one's nondominant hand at a human silhouette–shaped target twenty yards away.

"In my thirty-year career," White recalls, "a large part of my duties was training. It was something I took so seriously. I owed that to my people—to make their jobs safer and easier and ensure they're gonna get home to their families."

One more Tony White story: The man preached often about the importance of exiting our vehicles when making contact with people. Inside your truck or car, he emphasized, you were confined, vulnerable. One of his mantras: "You don't want your car to be your casket." Once you were outside the vehicle, it could be used for cover and concealment. This raised questions about shooting *through* our cover if the situation became dire. Could we effectively shoot through our vehicles or their windows and windshields?

White was determined to find out. After getting the go-ahead from his chief, he started planning a large training exercise, which began with a visit one morning to Nations

Towing south of Moab. There, he asked the proprietors if they might have a beat-up old pickup truck he could borrow "for a couple weeks."

"It may get a few bullet holes in it," he allowed. "And we're going to shoot the windshield out."

After he explained why he needed a truck, they were happy to loan him an old beater they had sitting out back. They even put a working battery in it for him.

His next visit was to Rick's, an auto glass store a few miles north on Highway 191. White asked that, instead of discarding windshields with minor damage—a small spiderweb or modest crack—they set them aside for him. Every week he'd go by and harvest another dozen or so windshields, all stacked nicely on a pallet by the good people at the shop. It wasn't long before he had a couple hundred windshields to work with.

One spring morning in 2009, we loaded the sacrificial pickup on a flatbed truck, along with all those windshields, and hauled everything up to Salt Lake City. Over the course of three days, a total of around seventy-five officers, myself included, engaged in a series of simulated gunfights. Earmuffed and begoggled—and having a blast, frankly—we shot at targets through the side windows, then the windshield. The purpose was to observe how the glass affected both the trajectory of the bullet and the impact it had upon striking the target.

Before the exercise, I might have hesitated to shoot through a car's door or window. The training proved, as

White put it later, that our prescribed duty rounds could reliably "penetrate intermediate to heavy barriers"—tempered auto glass and car doors, for example—with reliable accuracy and minimal "fragmentation."

White told me he'd run into some resistance planning that exercise. Some administrators on the non–law enforcement side of the agency questioned the value and cost of the exercise. "I was pretty stubborn," he remembers. "I said, 'No, this has the potential to save lives.'"

That specialized training was in addition to my own intensified regimen of physical fitness. No longer a river guide, I didn't have a source of built-in exercise—it was no longer part of my job. Or at least it wasn't a very big part. But in the year before our third child, Jag, was born, I started ramping up my fitness. I was swimming and lifting and running a few miles every other day or so. The odd thing is, if you asked me why, I couldn't have given you a specific reason.

We feel better when we're fit. So there's a health and, yes, vanity component. As a formerly doughy adolescent, I liked being a little more, well, *sculpted*. I wanted to keep the dad bod at bay. And part of it had to do with the high bar that Wendy set in our marriage. I felt compelled to at least be able to keep up with her on a run or bike ride.

But there was something else going on. For a reason that I couldn't articulate, I felt an urge, an imperative, to be in the best shape I possibly could. Like there was some goal or test—some unknown physical ordeal just over the horizon, where I couldn't see it. It was a premonition.

"We Needed to Get Away from Each Other"

This is from an interview with Lance Arellano's mother, conducted by detectives from the Grand County Sheriff's Office a day after the shooting:

DET. 1: When he left the house that afternoon, you guys were having an argument?

LANCE'S MOTHER: Yeah, I came home from work and just said, you know, I cannot.

DET. 1: What was he doing when you got home?

LM: He was out doing the chores, the chickens and stuff. We had the agreement he would keep the vehicles running, and he just wasn't doing it. I just snapped. I said, "Just go stay with [another family]. Just leave." He said fine. We needed to get away from each other. It was starting to feel like my ex-husband was living here. And I swore to myself I would never live like that again....

DET. 2: Is he a glass-half-full or half-empty guy?

LM: I think he's more the half-empty type. I think he was depressed. I think we were both depressed and neither one of us knew how to figure it out.

Chapter 5

BLINDSIDED

The sun was already setting around 5 p.m. on Friday, November 19, 2010. Daylight savings had ended twelve days before, and the shorter days still seemed like an affront. *How is it getting dark already?*

It is understood by all who know her that Wendy's mood is boosted by movement, some kind of workout. The posse of friends who stroll with her on hikes and promenades around the neighborhood refer to themselves as "Wendy's Walkers."

She was returning from just such a walk around the 'hood early that evening as I headed out for a second shift. Working a double would leave me pretty crispy for the rest of the weekend, but that time and a half is sweet.

These were the serene, halcyon days of early parenthood. After moving into the little house on Park Drive, we were warmly welcomed into our new community. Our lives took on a tranquil, blissful rhythm.

I'm joking, of course. Our daughter, Jayde, born three years after Stryder, was followed three years later by their baby brother, Jag. Bedlam and chaos reigned in our casa, but it was a good chaos. We embraced the anarchy, the mess—even celebrated it.

To make ends meet, I jumped on every overtime shift I could.

Wendy stepped onto the lawn that fateful evening just as I was coming out of the house. She wasn't wearing a jacket and remarked on how warm it was for mid-November. While she remembers saying "Have a good night," at no point during this rushed hello-goodbye—"ships passing in the night" is how she later described it—did either of us stop walking. I don't remember if I told her that I loved her.

Tony White and I had spent the day forty-odd miles northwest of town, patrolling the White Wash Sand Dunes Recreational Area, helping some Bureau of Land Management workers put up some border fencing, and reminding people to be courteous to others, to wear their helmets, stay on the trail, and steer clear of the wildlife, including the bighorn sheep grazing out there.

Now back at our regional office on the south side of Moab, we fixed on a game plan for our second shift. On this pleasant Friday night, we would be looking for parties. Our overtime was underwritten by a grant stipulating that, for this shift, we'd be focusing on the prevention of underage alcohol consumption—of which there was plenty, trust me, in the backcountry of Grand County. The goal was to go find the teenage drinkers, take their six-packs or bottles, and arrange a poignant reunion with their parents.

I'm the kind of ranger who tries to put the *peace* in *peace officer*. I keep it pretty low key, even when I'm citing someone. In the past, I've sidled up to a group around a campfire, stood next to them, then waited until they noticed my uniform. That's when I would smile and say, "Hey, how's everyone doing? Now I need to see some IDs." Sometimes I'll bust someone or write them a ticket and nonetheless get a handshake or a note from them later, thanking me for how I handled the situation. It's a reminder that most of the people we encounter are intrinsically good. Some of 'em just happen to be making bad choices at that moment.

White and I decided to split up for a few hours, do some recon, and check out some popular party spots. Later we'd team up and then make contact with any large groups we found. He headed south out of Moab for about nine miles, then took a left on Ken's Lake Road, which rose up from the valley floor to a Jeep trail called Steel Bender. I went north, crossing over the Colorado, then hair-pinning south, following the river on Potash Road, so named for the old potash mine fifteen serpentine miles down canyon.

After just two miles on Potash Road, road and river exit the valley through a vast aperture in the thousand-foot cliffs west of town. That passage, carved in the sandstone monolith over millions of years, is known by locals as the Portal. Once you're on the far side of the Portal, cell service and radio comms are very sketchy. I passed through the Portal, then went by Wall Street—not a street at all but a section of Wingate Sandstone popular with rock climbers drawn to its sheer cliffs. A mile past some roadside petroglyphs, across the Colorado from an especially dramatic succession of cliffs called the Tombstones, I took a loose right onto the dirt road that rises gradually to the Poison Spider Mesa trailhead.

As that road switchbacked into the parking lot, the headlights of my truck swept over a single sedan at the far end of the lot. I would later describe it as a silver Camry, but this was in fact a four-door Pontiac Grand Am—similar to the model Wendy was driving around at the time we got married. A car at the trailhead at this late hour could mean a hiker, mountain biker, motorbiker, or Jeeper was lost, injured, or worse, in the backcountry. I needed to take a look.

The driver had backed the car into a spot at the rear of the lot, close to the restrooms. The Grand Am's rear bumper was only a few feet from the rocks behind it. Twenty feet away, I stopped and put my F-150 pickup in park with the engine running. My headlights and white overhead lights stayed on.

I glanced at the Pontiac's plates and made a mental note: registration stickers were expired. After walking behind the car to jot down the plate number, I moved to the driver's side. Looking into the backseat, I saw a person sleeping.

I rapped with my knuckles on the left rear window once, then again. The figure stirred, sat up, then opened the door. He was a white male with dark, shaggy, medium-length hair. He had a blanket drawn over his shoulders.

I asked if he was OK, if he needed help. Yes, he replied, he was OK. He looked me in the eye as we spoke. It was a calm, civil conversation. He didn't seem upset or agitated. I told him he couldn't spend the night in the parking lot, but there were a bunch of campsites close by. We talked about the Kane Creek area, just across the river.

"Am I free to go?" he asked. I told him I needed to get some information from him, then he would be free to go. I asked for his ID. He didn't have it with him, he said. When I asked for his name, he said "Michael Oher," then gave me a fake date of birth.

That name sounded vaguely familiar, but I couldn't place it at the moment. This was a year after the release of the movie *Blindside*, about ex-NFL offensive tackle Michael Oher, who experienced homelessness as a teen, was raised by a Tennessee couple, and then became a football star.

I never saw *Blindside*, but I was about to get blindsided.

I walked back to my truck, where I intended to run his name and plate number.

I would've learned in the next few moments that the car's owner had been cited a dozen times over the last three years for misdemeanors ranging from theft and DUI to failure to comply, driving without insurance, and driving on a suspended license. Warrants had been issued for his arrest.

Walking toward my truck, I glanced back at the Grand Am. My truck lights were still on, so it wasn't pitch black. But it was dark enough that I couldn't see if the guy was moving. In the second before I reached the door, a shot rang out, and a slug tore through my left arm just below the shoulder, blowing up the humerus bone into a score of fragments. The momentum of that bullet spun me 180 degrees. Now looking back over my right shoulder, I saw him walking toward me,

NINE MIRACLES

his advance garishly illuminated by repeated muzzle flash. Three more shots hit me.

I consider a bullet-resistant vest part of my uniform. You wear the uniform, you wear the vest. Those three shots, a detective later told me, formed a "close pattern" in my back. One bullet got through. It ended up lodged against a vertebra in my lumbar region. That fusillade knocked me to the ground. Time slowed. The shooter kept advancing, bearing down until he was nearly standing over me, until he stood over me, still firing.

After several eternities, the shooting stopped. The desert went quiet. He turned to walk back to his car. He was leaving me for dead. He'd fired fifteen rounds and hit me with nine, not including the slug that was embedded in my wallet, tucked as usual in the right cargo pocket of my uniform pants, where it gave its life to save my femur.

Everything in my life came down to the choice I would make in the next moment. I could let go, check out. I mean, I was as good as gone, right? Surely no one could blame me if I chose then to slip the surly bonds of my wrecked body and proceed to the next realm—to whatever lies in store for us at the end of this life. Or I could push back against such a sad fate and see what happened.

It took about a half second to make that decision.

A friend of mine sometimes quotes his father, one George Newell Lewis, on the topic of not quitting, never giving in: "If people don't like you, that's OK; they can't whip you," he would say. "But if they can whip you, they can't kill you. But if they do kill you, they can't eat you. And if they eat you, you don't have to taste good." My chances of seeing another sunrise weren't looking really good in that moment. This gunman, whoever this guy was, might end up taking my life. But I wasn't going to taste good.

As he walked away, I took inventory. I didn't know I'd been shot with hollow-point slugs, designed to expand on impact, creating more tissue damage, and that I was now carrying shrapnel in my liver, small intestine, groin, both arms, and right hip. One bullet grazed the left ventricle of my heart. Another had pierced the lower lobe of my left lung. And there was the slug in the L2 region of my spine. I knew I had been shot and that my left arm was throbbing in pain. I didn't realize I was in such bad shape.

But I could move, I discovered. I could sit up. I could stand. And walk!

And so, to the gunman's surprise and disappointment, I did.

Well, I wasn't *walking* so much as I was lurching like a drunk. But I was upright and mobile. I was alive.

Now he was headed back toward the truck, intending, I surmised, to finish me off.

My training kicked in. I took cover on the far side of my Ford F-150. I'm not sure he was aware of this, but I had a gun too.

So I reached for my service weapon.

I reached for it again.

I reached for it a third time.

NINE MIRACLES

But my left arm was no longer taking requests from my brain. With its humerus bone shattered, the arm was now a flopping, useless meat sock, flailing around of its own volition. It even swung up once and clobbered me in the face. That's the kind of day I was having.

After trying several times to draw with my left hand, I had an epiphany: *You IDIOT, use your other hand. You've trained to do this.*

In my right hand, I held a flashlight, pen, and notebook. Please do not ask why I continued to cling to them while being shot repeatedly, for I have no idea. But now I dropped them and reached with my right hand for the .40-caliber Glock holstered on my left hip.

It was a slightly awkward, cross-body movement, made more so by all the new holes in my body. But I had practiced the maneuver, and now the "motor memory" kicked in. With my right hand, I drew my duty weapon. Now the playing field was, if not level, less slanted in his favor.

Gun in hand, I started to get my bearings. I retreated to the back of my truck, with the shooter crouched behind the front. I fired several times in his direction, but I struggled to get a clear shot. Time was not on my side. Throughout this deadly cat-and-mouse game, my vision was narrowing. I was on the verge of collapsing. I was bleeding out on my feet. So I shot through my cover.

The previous March, at a firearms training center called The Farm, I'd spent a day with a bunch of fellow rangers firing rounds through the windows and windshield of that poor sacrificial pickup truck, each bullet driving home the lesson: yes, these rounds will penetrate a car window, a car door—pretty much everything in the car but the engine block.

A few months after that training, I had a geeky inside-baseball conversation with my chief, Christopher Quick, about the caliber of bullets in our duty weapons and what those rounds could penetrate. I flashed back to that exchange while circling the F-150, warily eyeing the would-be cop killer. I began shooting at him through the truck's windows and both of its windshields, front and rear. Now he was on the defensive and had run out of ammo.

So had I, for the moment. I had two more magazines in my belt. Getting one of them in the Glock without the use of my left arm was going to be an adventure. The one-handed reload is a tricky operation and rarely needed—like an onside kick in football. But when you need it, you *really* need it. So it pays to practice.

After firing sixteen rounds, I stripped the spent magazine, dropped it to the ground, then reached for the full mag on my belt. I dropped it. No problem—that's why we carry a second spare magazine. Taking a bit more care this time, I grabbed the mag. Holding the gun between my knees, I pushed the full magazine into the handle of the Glock. So far, so good.

But I still had to transfer a bullet into the chamber. Normally, that's as simple as holding the gun in my left hand while "racking" the slide—pulling backward on it—with my right. To perform that operation one handed, I hooked the rear sights of the weapon on the truck bumper and then pushed down, successfully racking the slide and slamming a fresh round home. I was back in the fight.

When I popped up again, looking for him, he was still crouching behind the hood of my truck. I fired repeatedly in his direction. Increasingly discouraged, out of ammo, and possibly wounded himself, he retreated back to his car.

Now I advanced on him, striding to the truck's passenger-side mirror and squeezing off more rounds. I recall Lance speaking these words to me: "You got me." He suddenly raised his hands. I had him at gunpoint but stopped firing because I could see his hands.

By this time, the house lights were going down, and I began to lose consciousness. Stumbling backward, I ended up on my back, on the ground, ten or twelve feet behind my truck. When I regained consciousness, he and his car were gone. He thought I had died, is my best guess.

Around this time, a ready-mix truck rumbled into the parking lot and pulled alongside me, its cavernous drum spinning, and commenced pouring wet concrete on top of me. Or so it seemed at that moment. I felt a mounting, oppressive heaviness. I couldn't move.

This will sound like a moment from a Hallmark movie, but it happened, so I'm sharing it here: Looking up at the night sky, the beams of a near-full moon penetrating the low clouds like a flashlight behind a blanket, I thought of Wendy and our children, saw each of their faces. It happened in a flash, much more quickly than it just took me to describe it. But in that moment, I resolved to make it back to them, to be in their lives, to grow old with the woman I love, and to spoil our grandchildren. I would not "go gentle into that good night," to borrow from the Welsh poet Dylan Thomas. I would "rage, rage against the dying of the light."

I had not called out to the dispatcher before tapping on the gunman's window. No one knew where in the world I was. If I didn't get help, I would be dead within the hour. The good news: the radio in my truck, my connection to the outside world, was only thirty-five or so feet away. The bad news: it might as well have been the length of the Appalachian Trail. I couldn't walk, couldn't stand, couldn't even crawl.

Perhaps I could . . . roll? I started rolling. I would rotate onto my stomach, then take several breaths. I would roll onto my back, then recover with several breaths. And so on. I had bullets in most of my vital organs, but those wounds didn't hurt nearly as much as my poor left arm, which made kind of a clacking sound, like a bag of marbles, when it moved. Each time I rolled onto it, I felt a crunching, excruciating pain. It took me at least ten minutes, rolling over gravel and spent shell casings, to cover those thirty-five feet. But I got there.

For as long as I've been a ranger, I've always left the driver's side door wide open when contacting people in the backcountry. What appears to be an oversight—*Look, he left his door open*—is a precaution. You never know when you're going to have to get back inside or get out of the vehicle in a *hurry*. The truth is, I could not have told you, or my colleagues, why I always left the door open. I just did. It was an intuition that I honored, a hunch. I can't fully explain it.

NINE MIRACLES

If that door had been closed that night, I'm not sure how I would've opened it. I probably would've found some way to at least kneel and reach up and open it with my good arm. But that's not a sure thing. I'm glad I didn't have to find out. I'm glad the door was open. And I'm glad I keep the microphone low on the console.

After dragging myself to a sitting position, I leaned against the doorframe and reached with my right arm for the microphone that was, quite literally in that moment, a lifeline. I reached and stretched and groaned and got my hand on it.

But I didn't use it right away. I took a moment to rehearse in my head what I was going to say. This was drummed into us from our earliest days in basic training at the POST Academy: Your voice on the radio needs to be calm, clear, steady. Keep it short and to the point.

I was scared and alone and near death in the backcountry, but I didn't want to come across that way. I pushed the button on the side of the mic, identified myself by my call sign—two alpha six-nine—and spoke these words: "I've been shot. I'm at Poison Spider Mesa. Please help me."

The radio transmission on which my life depended would need to find its way to the antenna of the Bald Mesa Repeater, 15 miles east and 8,400 feet up in the La Sal Mountains. From there the signal would be relayed 140 miles northwest to the state's Consolidated Dispatch Center in Price, Utah, which would then bounce it 100 miles south to our local dispatcher in Moab. The shortest side of that obtuse triangle would be the trickiest. To get from my truck to Bald Mesa, the signal would have to get up and over the Tombstones, a set of nearby cliffs looming 500 feet over the river. All I could do now was hope. I lay down again, and the cement truck returned—that feeling of being encased.

It's odd what pops into your head when you're in "profound hemorrhagic shock," as one of my surgeons later put it. I remembered the gist of an article I'd read a few years earlier on the benefits of yogic breathing, also known by its Sanskrit name, *pranayama*. By slowing and deepening your breathing, you can lower your blood pressure and reduce your heart rate. And so, as I stared up at those clouds, I made that my job. Consciously, intentionally, I connected one breath to the next, to the next, to the next. *Just get to the next breath*, I told myself. If I linked enough breaths together, I'd be alive when help arrived. *If* help arrived.

On the far side of Moab, back by Ken's Lake, White had come across a vehicle of interest near an area known as Caves. No one was in that car, and no one was around. "Nothing remarkable," he recalled. "It just seemed very strange." He wanted me to come join him, "to expand the search area," as he put it. When he tried to reach me on the radio, he got no reply. White then dropped into a kind of bowl in the red rock that took him out of radio contact. After emerging from that dead zone, he recalls, he was thinking about me, wondering why I hadn't been in touch, when my voice came over the radio: "Price . . . [*inaudible shouting*] BEEN SHOT. I'm at Poison Spider Mesa. Please help me."

And that's when everything kicked into overdrive.

Grand County Deputy Sheriff Al Cymbaluk was on duty that night, working with Moab police officer Shaun Hansen as part of a Major Crimes Task Force focusing on narcotics trafficking. They were right in the middle of downtown Moab, in Cymbaluk's patrol car, when my call came in.

"I don't remember Brody's exact verbiage," Cymbaluk later said. "I do remember the anxiety in his voice." Ten and a half miles from the trailhead, when they heard my call come in, they made the drive in nine minutes and change. "I started to roll code immediately," he recalled, referring to Code 3, an emergency situation calling for increased speed, flashing lights, and a blaring siren. Once they were north of town, however, Cymbaluk shut down the siren box and overhead lights. "If the suspect was heading toward us," he explained, "I didn't want to give him a heads-up."

Cymbaluk and Hansen didn't know what to expect. They didn't know if the gunman had stuck around, if they were driving into an ambush. The moment they veered off Potash Road onto the dirt lane up to the parking lot, they would be exposed and vulnerable. "The suspect would clearly have the high ground," Cymbaluk stated. It was one of those situations "where you could go deliberate"—proceed slowly and with caution—"or go dynamic. . . . We chose dynamic because we knew Brody had been shot."

As it happened, Cymbaluk had been preparing for an upcoming SWAT training and had two rifles and two sets of body armor in his car. Hansen donned body armor as they drove.

As the dirt road switched back, or buttonhooked, as Cymbaluk said, "We saw Brody's headlights pointed toward the bathroom." Armed with a rifle, Hansen got out of the car and peeled left, then right, scanning for the gunman. Cymbaluk drove to within four car lengths of my truck, then approached me on foot, also carrying a rifle.

His vehicle would serve as cover "in case I needed to engage the suspect right there," recounts Cymbaluk. "And Hansen would have another angle from his location. . . . I rolled in a little bit closer and popped out of my vehicle," he recalls. "And that's when I saw Brody next to his truck."

It wasn't until the spring of 2024 that I watched dashboard video of the incident taken from Cymbaluk's vehicle. In it, he kneels, telling me, "We got an ambulance on the way, boss."

I reply, "Good," then begin blurting info between ragged, labored breaths: "Silver Camry. Expired plates. Think I shot him. . . . First three [characters] A-1-2." I've forgiven myself for identifying the Grand Am as a Camry. Those sedans, equally nondescript, do look a lot alike. And I nailed the first three numbers of the license plate, A-1-2.

"Considering the extent of Brody's injuries," Cymbaluk later said, "it was just amazing, his composure, the way he held it together." Cymbaluk slipped a mask onto my face to deliver supplemental oxygen. He kept me engaged and conscious, then delivered this news: "Ambulance is here, brother. Ambulance is here."

"He Wasn't Trying to Shoot to Get Away; He Was Trying to Kill"

LANCE'S MOTHER: Was the police officer on the ground or in the car?

DET. 1: They found him beside his truck on the ground. And he's hit, six to seven times.

DET. 2: And they are very close groups.

DET. 1: [Most shootings of police officers] are "spray and pray," hope that you hit someone. The individual that shot this officer was a very good shot, and he was very tactical; he used the truck for cover. And I'm sad to say he was pursuing the officer. He wasn't trying to shoot to get away; he was trying to kill. And we feel that the only reason the officer [didn't get] one in the head is that Lance ran out of ammunition.

. . .

LM: They said he's been shot three times, but he's got six rounds in him?

DET. 1: Who said he was shot three times?

LM: That's what I'm hearing on the news.

DET. 2: You can't believe that.

. . .

DET. 1: But anyway, what do you think of Lance as a person?

LM: [*Whispering*] He's a good kid.

DET. 1: What?

LM: [*Louder, defiant*] He's a good kid.

Chapter 6

"NOT ON MY WATCH"

Because she was on call that Friday night, Moab EMT Michelle Steele brought her pager to the auditorium at Grand County High School, where the drama club was crushing its performance of *Fiddler on the Roof*. Sometime during act 2, the pager buzzed. "Please get to the ambulance shed," she was told, "and await further instructions." Before she even arrived, the crew was told to get to Poison Spider Mesa.

I knew Michelle a little through her husband, Jeff, then the lead maintenance worker at Dead Horse Point State Park. We took them down Westwater Canyon in a raft once and had a blast. By the time that ambulance rolled into the parking lot, Michelle knew that I was the guy on the ground.

In the previous ten days, she'd been out on three grim calls. She responded to a report of a "baby in distress." That eleven-month-old died the next morning, "probably from being shaken," she said. "I had a thirteen-year-old hit by a vehicle as he was running across [Highway] 191. I had an individual at the Denny's, a drug deal gone bad; he was stabbed underneath the armpit." Both those patients died as well. "And then Brody's happened, and I told myself I was not gonna let that happen to him."

Phil Mosher is a volunteer firefighter by day and runs ambulance by night. (That's the preferred expression in EMT circles: they say, "I run ambulance" rather than "I drive an ambulance.") So it's not surprising that he was sitting around the living room with his family after dinner with one ear on the scanner. "I heard this scratchy call come through, and it was Brody," he remembers. "I was out the door and headed to the ambulance shed before [the dispatcher] paged it out."

Due to the abbreviated nature of my distress call, they had no way of knowing whether I was in the parking lot at Poison Spider or somewhere up the trail. In case I was in the backcountry, Phil made the call to roll in the county's 4×4 off-road ambulance, which, despite its boxy appearance, hauls ass. With fellow EMT Mike Ericksen at the wheel, they made the ten-mile drive from shed to trailhead in ten minutes—and that includes a brief delay: sheriff's deputies held them up for a minute outside of town while they made sure the road was clear.

Veering right onto the dirt road leading to the trailhead, the EMTs were heartened to see Officer Shaun Hansen scanning the canyon, rifle in hand. It gave them some comfort, Phil remembers, to know they didn't need to watch their backs.

In the dashcam video, Phil and Michelle pile out of the truck. After tiptoeing around a constellation of spent shells—not wanting to disturb the crime scene—Michelle approaches me from the north. She toggles between tender expressions of encouragement—"Hey, buddy, how you doing?"—and brusque reports and instructions to the crew, all while cutting off my clothes with special shears:

"Get on the phone and get CareFlight *now.*"

"How's your breathing, baby?"

"We're loadin' and goin'!" (That is, it was a clear-cut "load-and-go" case—a patient in need of immediate transport, as opposed to a "stay and stabilize.")

Seeing wounds in my left chest, they rolled me on my right side. "At that point I saw two more gunshots in his back," Michelle recounts. "The only logical thing I could think of was they went through the vest."

They used a backboard to relay me to the collapsible gurney. The blood made it hard to lift me up. "His leg is slippery," Phil told Al Cymbaluk. "Lock hands, go underneath."

As Ericksen did his best to break the Potash Road land speed record getting us to the hospital, Michelle and Phil worked on me in the back, using trauma dressings to plug the wounds they could see. While kneeling beside me, Phil extended one of his legs, creating a temporary support to hold up my dangling left arm while Michelle wrapped it. Meanwhile, he was searching high and low for a place to stick an IV. They needed to get fluids and blood in me.

"Usually," says Phil, "when you do IVs in an ambulance, you want to go for one of the upper extremities." With bullet wounds in either arm, that seemed like a bad idea. You don't want to put the IV near a bullet hole, Phil explains, "because then all the fluids you're pushing in kinda push right out." Makes sense.

He finally succeeded in sinking an IV somewhere down near my ankle and got some fluids in. Why the ankle? What about all my other veins? "They'd all collapsed. Because you had pretty much bled out."

I don't recall this, but Michelle tells me I grabbed her arm at one point—must've been with my right hand—and asked, "Am I going to die?"

"Not on my watch," she replied.

Ericksen got us back to Moab in seven minutes, reversing expertly into the ambulance bay at Allen Memorial Hospital, only a quarter mile from our house, where Wendy was probably crocheting or ensconced in a book after putting the kids to bed.

When they opened the ambulance doors, Phil was shaken by what he saw. "I've been on crashes, I've seen people in really bad shape, but I'd never seen that much blood run out of the back of an ambulance." He didn't think I was going to make it, and I don't take that personally. "When you see that many holes in somebody and that much blood coming out . . ." He didn't finish the thought.

As the ER crew converged on me, Michelle returned to the back of the ambulance. Like Lady Macbeth, she tried in vain to clean up all the blood. While she was cleaning, she says, "That's when it hit me, what had just happened. That's when it hit me, this was Brody's blood." She wept and made a decision. After twelve and a half years as an EMT, she was finished. She transferred a couple patients from Moab to Salt Lake. But she never went on another emergency call.

Chapter 7

ALLEN MEMORIAL'S FINEST HOUR

Even before my unscheduled pit stop at our local hospital that night, Wendy didn't much care for the place. "It was creepy," she recalls. "There was this green glow in the hallways at night. It was like going to a haunted house."

That assessment, widely shared around town, would have injured the feelings of Frank Lloyd Wright, who came up with the "Usonian" style of design that characterized Allen Memorial Hospital, a practical, streamlined, single-story building made with native materials. Celebrated as Moab's "state-of-the-art" medical center when it opened in 1957, Allen Memorial had reached the end of its lifespan in late 2010.

Among its quirks and shortcomings: to enter after hours, visitors passed *through* the emergency room to reach the reception area—an awkward layout that took some getting used to for Dr. Patrick Scherer: "If somebody came in sick, you had fifteen family members sitting smack-dab in the middle of the ER. Kind of a real strange setup."

In addition to being oddly configured, Allen Memorial was outdated, underresourced, and increasingly inadequate for Moab's growing population. A few months later, on

Valentine's Day, there would be a ribbon cutting to celebrate the opening of the gleaming new Moab Regional Hospital.

But on this night, three months before it closed for good, fifty-four-year-old Allen Memorial would have, arguably, its finest hour. (I will admit to some bias here, as mine was the life that was saved.)

Part of it was dumb luck, as we shall see. But the biggest reason I survived that first fraught hour was the roster of unsung all-stars who happened to be working that night and whose cool, quiet competence turned Murphy's Law on its head: everything that could go right, did.

Case in point: Dr. Scherer, a highly regarded emergency medicine specialist, was on duty in the ER that night. A Pittsburgh native who spent five years in the navy, Scherer was in the service during Operation Desert Storm in 1991 but wasn't called overseas. The most trauma he saw during that period, Scherer says, was in Jacksonville, Florida, where he completed his residency and worked many rotations at the University of Jacksonville hospital's ER, which was often referred to as a "Knife and Gun Club." On one memorable Fourth of July, he remembers, they treated "six or seven" gunshot victims in a single night. Moab proved to be much different. "We see a lot of mild to moderate trauma," he says. "Broken bones, lacerations, motorcycle and ATV accidents."

According to EMT Phil Mosher, a typical Moab call involves "somebody going out, crashing something, falling off something. We don't see too many gunshots." The ER crew at Allen Memorial had been told to expect a patient who'd been shot but had been given no other details. "Because it's Moab," says Scherer, "you thought, OK, somebody shot himself in the toe with a .22."

Also on duty that night was ER nurse Matt McCune, who remembers people "congregating around the scanner," waiting for any updates.

Once through the Portal, that thousand-foot cliff interposed between Moab proper and the canyon where I was shot, the ambulance was able to radio more specifics to the ER: the incoming patient had suffered multiple gunshot wounds. This news triggered a "Level 1" trauma call—a kind of "all-hands-on-deck" alert for certain hospital personnel. The operating room crew was summoned, along with extra nurses and X-ray technicians. Already at the hospital—and this was a stroke of excellent fortune for me—was Jack Frayne, a lab tech who quickly determined my blood type and began shuttling to the ER the bags, or "units," of blood the nurses needed to infuse into me.

Even with that heads-up from the ambulance, says Scherer, "I don't think we understood the gravity of the situation until he got here." They kept finding new bullet holes, he recalls: "It was like, 'Oh, there's another one. And another! And another. And every one of 'em in a bad place.'"

On this night, with no general surgeon available, I would not go under the knife at Allen Memorial. The goal was to get me stabilized, then transferred to a bigger hospital. That meant a forty-minute helicopter ride to St. Mary's Regional

Hospital in Grand Junction, Colorado, sixty-five miles by air to the northeast.

Upon realizing the extent of my injuries, the ER called St. Mary's to request a "life flight" on its chopper. That bird, they were informed, was already en route. For that I had my supervisor, Tony White, to thank.

The first thing Tony did after emerging from that rock bowl and hearing my distress call was to let dispatch know he was headed to Poison Spider. The next thing he did was request an air ambulance. He had no idea how badly shot up I was, yet he summoned the chopper with zero hesitation. Not surprisingly, he'd planned for such a scenario: "I'd always rehearsed, if we've got an officer down, whether it's a snowmobile accident or a vehicle crash or some kind of shooting, whatever, we're gonna get a helicopter in the air, out of an abundance of caution."

That would tick off a bucket-list item for me: as I often mentioned to Wendy when choppers thwacked their way over our house on their way to Allen Memorial some four hundred yards away, I'd only ever been on a helicopter one time, as a small child, and I had little memory of it. I wanted another ride on a chopper, albeit under better circumstances.

Nonetheless, to stabilize me for that flight, the Moab team needed to get a lot of blood into me—and fast. "We didn't have a surgeon, so there was nothing I could do to stop the bleeding, other than direct pressure," Scherer recalls. My heart rate was a stratospheric 180 beats per minute—a symptom, Scherer concluded, of "critical shock." That severe tachycardia led him to believe that I was bleeding out. "So it was *blood, blood, blood, and transfer,*" said Scherer, distilling the mission into five words.

How would they get all that blood in me? Phil had managed to get an IV in my left foot on the ambulance, despite my collapsing veins—"a great stick," Matt McCune recalls with admiration. A crackerjack RN named Annie Relph got another IV in my other foot once I got to the ER. While helpful, those small-bore catheters allowed for only limited flow rates.

Having arrived freshly fenestrated—full of new holes—I would now have a front-row seat as my new friends put still more holes in me. Matt sent Phil back out to his ambulance to retrieve a device called an IO bone injection gun, a go-to for EMTs when traditional intravenous methods aren't cutting it.

IO stands for *intraosseous*, Latin for "within the bone." About the size of a Dremel, the IO gun is basically a glorified power tool that drills a hole in the bone—in my case, my right tibia, just below the knee—to sink a catheter in the marrow, through which infused fluids can quickly reach "central circulation."

I remember Phil augering into my leg bone—it produced the same acrid, burned enamel smell as a dentist drilling for a cavity. Yes, I felt every second of it. In the rush to get me stabilized, it was later explained to me, there wasn't sufficient time to apply lidocaine. As the drill sunk deeper, I envisioned a pair of lumberjacks at either end of a two-man saw, trying to take off my leg. But the pain from the drill was a light appetizer for the main course of agony that was served when they started pushing those fluids through the bone marrow. That hurt more than getting shot. It wasn't even close.

Meanwhile, McCune was scanning and scrutinizing me like a wildcatting oil prospector looking for another place to sink a well—or, in this case, a catheter. My left arm, "a floppy mess," in his words, was out of the question. After peeling back the bandage just below my right elbow, where a bullet had gouged out a melon-ball-sized hunk of flesh, he noticed that the nearby vein was unharmed: "So I just sunk a big ol' fat IV in him—a fourteen-gauge. It's the biggest IV we have, and one of the two we used to get blood into him."

Oddly, alarmingly, there were times when the nurses tried to take my blood pressure, but it was too low to register on their instruments. "He remained conscious the entire time," says McCune, "but didn't always have recordable vital signs." "How was he still conscious, in that case?" a reporter asked McCune a few years back. "I have no answer to your question," he replied. "For Brody to take the amount of injury he did and come back from it—that's not something that was in my hands, or the doctors' hands. That was between Brody and his Maker."

My focus, on that gurney at Allen Memorial, was on my job: linking breaths together. I was struggling, and Dr. Scherer feared I was on the way out. "Brody kept saying, 'I can't breathe, I can't breathe,' but his chest X-rays and his

ALLEN MEMORIAL'S FINEST HOUR

lungs were fine," he remembers. Blood carries oxygen from our lungs to the rest of our body. I was suffocating, Scherer surmised, because I didn't have enough blood. "I don't know whether he felt this," Scherer would later say, "but he looked like someone who had impending doom, like, 'I'm going to die.'"

I was kept alive by what amounted to a bucket brigade from the hospital's modest blood bank to my bedside. Thanks to the quick work of Jack Frayne, they knew my blood type was A positive. That was another stroke of luck. Those of us with A positive are compatible with all other blood types. That meant I could take any bag in the fridge. Which I did. By the time they were ready to wheel me out to the helicopter, McCune and Mosher and Relph and others had squeezed fourteen bags of blood into me. They put the hospital's last two bags on my chest before wheeling me out to the chopper.

"That's just a ridiculous amount of blood," says McCune. "Never again in my career will I put that much blood into a human being." There's a protocol for mass transfusions. But there's no way they could have followed it that night, considering the urgency of the moment and the limitations of Allen Memorial. "It's kind of unorthodox to just give that much blood, without also giving him platelets and fresh frozen plasma," says Scherer. But those products were lacking at this facility. So they kept squeezing packed red blood cells into me. As Scherer puts it, "We really didn't have any other choice."

It wasn't hectic, frantic, frenetic—not like some ER scenes you might see on medical dramas like *ER* or *Chicago*

Hope. In his experience, McCune says, the louder it is, the more chaos there is, the less gets done. The ER that night "wasn't people scrambling around and yelling. It was controlled. Scherer was very much running the room." Communication was strong in every direction. The crew was a well-oiled machine. As Scherer recalls, "This was one of those situations where I didn't have to say a whole lot to the team. Everyone just did their job, without me having to bark orders or anything like that. . . . For me, the hardest part was talking to Brody's wife."

Chapter 8

"IS HE GOING TO DIE?"

After our glancing, garden-variety goodbye earlier that evening—*ships passing in the night*—Wendy fed the kids, read to them, and put them to bed. She cleaned the kitchen and packed for her road trip the next day: she was driving eight-month-old Jag up to the children's hospital in Salt Lake to have his heart and kidneys scanned. Jag's fine now, but as a baby, he had some issues they wanted to keep an eye on.

She was primed for an hour or two of that rarest of commodities, "Wendy Time," when her phone buzzed. It was our friend Janel Arbon, who said without preamble, "Do you want me to come over to watch the kids?" Arbon's voice was strained. She sounded off. Puzzled, because she didn't need coverage, as far as she knew, Wendy replied, "Umm, no, I'm good."

Janel had gotten the news about me from her husband, Jeff, a highway patrolman who'd heard it over the radio. Now it dawned on her that Wendy didn't know yet. "I'll just come over," she said and got off the phone.

A minute or so later, there was a knock on the door. There loomed the figure of my boss, Tim Smith, who asked

Wendy if she needed him to watch the kids. Why was everyone offering to babysit all of a sudden? What was going on?

Tim told her I'd been shot, that it was serious, and that I would soon be life-flighted to Grand Junction. Wendy cut to the chase: "Is he going to die?" She wanted to know if she should wake the kids up so they could say goodbye to their father. Tim told her he didn't know, emphasizing that *she* needed to get to the hospital right away. Implicit in his urgent tone: I might not be alive when she got there.

Before driving over, Tim had reached out to a friend of his who is a bishop in our church. While not a Latter-day Saint himself, Tim thought it might be helpful to Wendy if the bishop was present when he broke the news. But when he called, his friend didn't pick up. "The one time I actually needed a Mormon bishop," Tim now feels free to wisecrack, "I couldn't find one."

The truth is, Tim wanted the guy's help in case Wendy broke down or became distraught. But there was no breakdown, no collapse. No wailing and gnashing of teeth. She received the news, absorbed it, "and then it was like, OK, she had a job to do," Tim remembers. "And she went inside to get her jacket and car keys."

People would comment often, in the weeks and months ahead, on Wendy's calm, measured demeanor in the wake of this cataclysm. They were saying (without saying), "Where are the tears? Where is the hysteria, the anguish?" One of the doctors who operated on me the night I was shot had given her a grim update, then misinterpreted her even-keeled response. As he put it later, "I just remember thinking, 'This woman has no idea. She seems so calm and put together . . . I don't think she realizes how close she was to losing her husband tonight.'"

Of course Wendy realized. She'd spoken to Dr. Scherer and Matt McCune. They'd leveled with her. She knew it was a coin flip if I'd make it to sunrise. It's simply not in her nature to "freak out," in her words. She's too strong mentally. "I don't think I'm mentally strong," she remarks, reading that description over my shoulder. (In addition to being mentally strong, she can be a tad contrarian.) "I just don't freak out in emergencies." Which, if you think about it, is a fine definition of "mentally strong."

In a poem to his son, Rudyard Kipling extols the sort of person able "to keep your head when all about you / Are losing theirs."

And that, friends, is Wendy's essence distilled to a verse of iambic pentameter. That quality is one of the reasons I love her—and one of the reasons she's a superb river guide. And therein lies a story I've decided to share now, because it will help the reader understand my wife more fully. We'll return to the haunted hospital in due time.

In early July 1999, a few months before we got married, Wendy went down the Colorado when the whitewater was big and gnarly. A rafting company in town was running an all-women's trip down the river and wanted only female guides. The bosses at Western River Expeditions volunteered

Wendy, who is excellent in an oar rig. She took the job but was nervous about it. They were going down Cataract Canyon.

The Colorado below Moab is a smooth ribbon, wending its way through the aptly named Meander Canyon before merging, some sixty miles south, with the Green River. The Confluence, as that spot is known, doubles the force of the river and marks the start of Cataract Canyon, a forty-six-mile defile through Canyonlands National Park containing fourteen miles of Class IV and V rapids strewn, during peak flows, with perilous pour-overs and voracious "holes" on the far sides of rocks and boulders. As water rushes over the obstacle, it flows back on itself, creating a hydraulic vortex, or "hole." Wendy had rowed Cataract when it was running at fifteen thousand cubic feet per second—a medium-level flow. This week it was ripping at fifty thousand cubic feet per second. She'd never *seen* it that big, let alone rowed it.

Wendy and her eight argonauts approached Capsize, a tricky rapid whose rock obstacles resemble a baseball diamond. On this cranking day on the Colorado, the pitcher's mound, home plate, and all the bases were huge boiling holes waiting to snatch and flip a raft. But instead, they had a glorious, sweet run through it, catching the side of home plate but emerging otherwise unscathed. Their luck would not hold.

In the days before the trip, she'd talked to fellow guides and studied video of specific rapids provided by the National Park Service. On this huge and thunderous day on the river,

"IS HE GOING TO DIE?"

she was struggling to recognize familiar features. The water was so high and furious that it was submerging them.

At one point, just above the rapid Big Drop 2, she realized she needed to cut hard to her left or risk the wrath of a nasty pour-over called Little Niagara. Big Drop 2 is what it sounds like. The river drops in elevation, and the water picks up speed and pours over house-size rocks that create a waterfall effect. These monsters can turn a boat inside out if caught on the downstream side or base of these obstacles. Rapids are rated more on how difficult it is to navigate through them than their size. The big drops are a combo of both. There are three big drops within Cataract Canyon.

Laying into her oars, she steered clear of that maelstrom only to have the boat pulled toward a hole created by a colossal obstacle called Marker Rock, a duplex-sized landmark that on this day was engulfed and obscured by the swollen, angry Colorado.

Wendy rowed crew at the U and rhapsodizes sometimes about getting into this rarefied zone with her boatmates, "when you get the swing going and everyone's in sync and there's nothing like it, you go so fast." It's a sight to behold when she's rowing full go. Oars in hand, she will start a stroke down by her ankles and pull with her legs and core and arms clear up to her clavicles. She was generating that kind of wattage, climbing the near-vertical face of a forty-foot wave created by a giant hydraulic—and had *alllll*most punched through it—when "Mother Nature flicked a finger," as she says, flipping the raft and its nine occupants back into the hole. No shame in that—plenty of boats get upended in such big water. As Wendy was told by guides from another company that night while they exchanged harrowing stories at the campsite, "We all flipped in Big Drop 2." It was that kind of day.

More interesting to me were her actions and instincts once they were in the drink. Like all Western River guides, she's certified in swift water rescue. When the raft flips, they're trained to ride it upside down through the rapids. Wendy tried riding on top but was tossed off three times while navigating a different monster wave called Red Wall and the tail waves beyond it. She ended up in the water with her clients, clinging to the "chicken line" that goes around the boat. Amid this chaos, she counted heads and was one passenger short. Sue, a spear-fisher woman and badass in her own right, had chosen to ride in an air pocket under the raft. It took Wendy a bit longer to find her.

They were headed for a fearsome rapid called Satan's Gut when Wendy shouted, "When I yell 'Swim!' let go of the boat and swim as fast as you can!" When the raft stalled briefly in the current, she gave the command, and they all swam toward a calm pocket on the left bank called Thank God Eddy. One woman, gripped with fear, was floating but not swimming. Wendy grabbed her by the lifejacket and sidestroked them both to safety.

Once they were all on the riverbank, a third woman, "in full-on shock," Wendy recalls, began to panic. To snap her out of it, Wendy slapped her. Not out of anger. She just needed to give the woman a reset. It worked. Everyone calmed down.

"IS HE GOING TO DIE?"

They found the boat in an eddy, where Wendy climbed across some floating logs and clipped her throw rope to the frame. Then they pulled it ashore, a feat far more herculean than it sounds. The eddy had served as a giant Oster blender. The women pulled three tree trunks, between eighteen and twenty feet long, from between the raft's floor and its frame. Two of three oars were wrecked, one bent ninety degrees. Another was missing its blade, its shaft "peeled back like a flower," recalls Wendy. After a makeshift repair of that oar, Wendy made a clean run through Big Drop 3. They all made it to camp in Dark Canyon and exchanged harrowing survival stories with the guides from an outfit called Adventure Bound.

People react differently in times of crisis. Wendy is the calmest, most level-headed person I know. She doesn't shout, doesn't do histrionics. She understands that outward displays of emotion—yelling, crying, becoming hysterical, placing blame—are not helpful in the moment. She accepts her new reality and makes a plan.

That said, when she got in her car, before driving to the hospital, she sobbed on the steering wheel. I mean, she's a tough *chica* but not a cyborg! "I had, like, a two-second freak-out," allows Wendy, who then called her father to let him know what was going on—but also just to hear his voice in that moment. That call ended just as she pulled up to Allen Memorial.

Wendy used a different entrance to the hospital than the doors I'd been pushed through. "I'm walking down this hallway, and it's totally quiet, and the weird fluorescent lights are flickering," she recollects. "I don't know where the emergency room is. I don't know where you go to see people when they've been shot." The first person she met was Mike Johnson, a nurse at the hospital who is also a friend from church. He directed her to the ER.

If Scherer and ER nurses McCune and Relph recall a calm, orderly scene, Wendy remembers it differently: "I went down the hall, and people were freaking out of their minds, crying. There were a ton of police officers and Brody's bosses, and I was wondering, *How am I the last person to know?*"

They brought Wendy to my bedside briefly. "He was lying on the table, and he was semiconscious, had all these tubes coming out of him, and there's ten thousand people around him trying to do stuff." It was clear that my left arm was a wreck, but she couldn't see my other wounds. It might not have mattered if she could. "Blood and guts don't bother me," says Wendy. "I don't think I was that horrified or anything. I was like, 'What am I supposed to do, just stand here?'"

She asked Johnson to give me a blessing before they loaded me on the chopper. It's common in our faith for a "priesthood holder" to place their hands on the head of one who is ill or otherwise in need of special comfort or healing and speak words of encouragement to carry them through the challenge. We're still not sure how he did it, but Johnson then switched into guerrilla minister mode, maneuvering his way—without asking anyone's permission—past

"IS HE GOING TO DIE?"

Scherer and through the nurses and other personnel, then placed a hand on my head and said a brief prayer. I don't remember it, but I'm grateful. Who knows, maybe it was Johnson's stealth blessing that put me over the top that night.

Someone said, "Did the wife make it? Is his wife here?" not realizing Wendy was ten feet away. When they found out who she was, she was taken to a room to speak with Scherer. He expressed surprise. "You're really married to him?" he asked. "You're doing pretty well."

"She was amazing," Scherer recalls. "She was obviously superconcerned, but she wasn't hysterical. She wanted to know the facts." He didn't sugarcoat my condition, letting Wendy know there was a chance I might not make it through the night. By this time, they'd decided to knock me out and intubate me—that is, insert a tube into my mouth and down my trachea—for the helicopter flight to St. Mary's.

Before the anesthesiologist knocked me out, Scherer told Wendy it would be a good idea for her to spend a few minutes by my side. He didn't say, because it was understood, that this might be the last time we saw each other. As nurses and others buzzed and hovered around her, Wendy gazed into my eyelids because I wouldn't open them. It was all I could do to focus on breathing. She said, "Hey, Brod, I guess you're finally gonna get that helicopter ride." Recalling the moment years later, she added, "I think I said 'I love you,' but I was like, dying"—figuratively, not literally—"because I hate being mushy or affectionate in front of people. And there were people everywhere, climbing all over us."

As I said, Dr. Scherer wasn't particularly bullish that night on my chances of living to a ripe old age. He wasn't sure I'd make it to Grand Junction. Relph, the ER nurse who squeezed blood into me that night, got a different vibe. Her gut told her I was going to make it. "Not because you looked good," she told me later, "but because you just had this will to live." She says, "I don't remember thinking, 'He's going to die.' But I do remember thinking, 'He needs to get over there'—to Grand Junction—'*now*.'"

No one had a better night than McCune, who later switched over to working for the county's Emergency Medical Services "running ambulance." (Now he's back in the ER, working graveyard shifts.) After the chopper left that night, he did something he hadn't done in thirteen years. "I went outside and bummed a smoke off one of the cops. Smoked a menthol cigarette and asked myself, 'What the f— just happened?'"

The people who work in ERs are good at compartmentalizing or walling off the blood and trauma they see on the job most days. If they're not good at it, after a while, they find something else to do. McCune has that knack. But seeing me in that condition stayed with him for a while, he's told me. "Not because it was a shooting," he says, "but because it was the shooting of someone I knew and had a connection with."

After he'd helped clean up the ER, finished his charting, and got to the end of his shift, McCune drove home. He remembers standing beside the crib of his eleven-month-old son. What was he feeling just then? "What I felt was this very heavy appreciation for life. And how fragile it is."

I went into the ER a year and a half later. What ailed me wasn't as serious this time around, though it hurt almost as much. I had a couple kidney stones I couldn't pass. And if you think that's too much information, just be glad I'm sparing you a fuller account of the bullet that nicked my scrotum, causing swelling in the area so dramatic that for a good two weeks, it had to be supported—swaddled, you might say—in a makeshift sling my nurses called "the hammock."

It was a slow morning in the ER when I came in with the kidney stones. After I was diagnosed, McCune and I stepped outside for a half hour. He asked me what happened that night at Poison Spider. I asked him what happened that night in the ER. As he shared his story, I felt a wave of gratitude and told him as much. What he said to me in return made me feel pretty good: "We can talk about what the doctors did, but the reason you're here is you didn't quit at any point along the way. You got ambushed. Then you stood up and got back in the fight. From the time that jerk shot you to this day right here, you've never quit. That's the single biggest factor in your outcome. That's why you're still here."

Chapter 9

"IF YOU WAKE UP MY KIDS, I'LL KILL YOU"

Wendy did wonder, during her drive home from Allen Memorial and in the days to come, if she might soon be a widow. Wendy being Wendy, she would push that thought from her mind and control the things she could control. At the moment, she needed to get home to pack and then drive to Grand Junction, 65 miles by helicopter but closer to 120 by car. She and Jag were already packed for a two-day trip, so she was expecting a quick turnaround.

Then she saw all the cars lining the street and the crowd outside our house, which was overrun with neighbors and friends, a good number of whom had driven directly from *Fiddler on the Roof*, after watching students belt out such numbers as "If I Were a Rich Man" and "To Life." It was a touching, textbook demonstration of how people in a close-knit community come together in times of crisis. They show up.

It was also a complete circus. The night I got shot was the night Wendy came to understand how many people in our town listen to the police scanner as a pastime. "That's how everyone found out before I did," she says. "And they all showed up at our house. There were people on the lawn, people at the front door. I had to push through them to get inside." Next, Wendy warned the visitors, many of whom were in tears, "Be *quiet*! You *have* to get it together. If you wake up my kids, I'll kill you."

As our dear friends Janel Arbon and Jennifer Taylor and others attended to Wendy, they ran interference, shared what little information they had, shushed people—"The kids are asleep!"—and also grappled with their own powerful emotions. Janel's husband, Jeff, you may recall, was the guy who had my job before becoming a state trooper. Now Arbon was beating herself up a bit, applying the tortured reasoning that if she hadn't given us a heads-up when the ranger job opened up, I wouldn't be on a ventilator right now. Taylor couldn't shake the ominous feeling that Wendy would be a single mom within days, if not hours. Both felt a powerful imperative to get Wendy out the door, into the car, and on the road to Grand Junction so she could be at my bedside if and when I checked out.

But Wendy goes at Wendy's pace. Always. Navy SEALs abide by a mantra, especially when the stakes are highest: "Slow is smooth, smooth is fast," a reminder that efficiency and speed come from deliberate, intentional actions. They rush less to achieve more. Wendy's like that, and on this fraught night, it was driving her friends around the bend. At one point, Janel remembers, Wendy sat down on the couch to talk to some people: "I was thinking, 'What the hell are you doing? You need to get out the door!'"

When Wendy finally did hit the road, she was riding shotgun with our buddy Jason Taylor—Jennifer's spouse—behind the wheel of his trusty Honda Pilot. Jason is yet another ex-river guide who also happens to have been our boss at the end of our guiding careers. He also "ran ambulance" for a dozen years and was an EMT in 2010.

He wasn't on call that night but remembers hearing the wail of the ambulance siren on its way out of town. Usually, that would prompt him to flip on the scanner to find out what was going on. On this night, he didn't. A half hour or so later, the landline in the kitchen rang, and it was Arbon with the scary news. The Taylors lived a few blocks from Allen Memorial, and Jason got there about a minute after me. He still remembers the sight of that jacked-up off-road ambulance, "blood still dripping out the back." (EMT Mosher would return with a fire engine to hose the ambulance bay down.)

Jason T. and Wendy started their journey to St. Mary's Hospital in Grand Junction, where I would spend the night on an operating table. Arbon was behind them, driving Wendy's car. As they motored north, Moab police and Grand County sheriff's vehicles poured into and out of town, their gaudy lights illuminating the night sky. Helicopters circled overhead, their searchlights crisscrossing the high desert.

They were stopped repeatedly at checkpoints that had already been set up. Each time, the car was stopped and given a cursory search. When they approached the third or fourth such checkpoint, Jason shouted out the window to the deputies, "This is the officer's wife—we're not stopping!" Those cops sent word to checkpoints ahead: let the Honda Pilot through.

"It was like a movie," Wendy remembers. "It didn't seem real." The reality was dawning on her that this emergency in our family didn't belong to just our family. Their charitable and protective instincts awakened, friends, neighbors, fellow church members, and strangers from across the state, the American West, the country, the *continent*, and as far as South Africa would take an interest in our situation. That outpouring of generosity and goodwill was deeply touching and remains one of the highlights of my life, a reminder that there's so much more good in the world than the few bad things that get highlighted on the news.

In practical terms, it meant frequent interruptions, intrusions, and disruptions for our family, most of which would fall on the shoulders of the woman riding beside Taylor as they pushed ninety-five miles per hour on I-70 toward Grand Junction. (Rocketing west the next day on his way home, Taylor was pulled over for speeding. He played the "I'm buddies with Brody Young" card and was not ticketed!)

The challenges that Wendy had already taken on in her life—overcoming her extreme shyness and bringing three very difficult pregnancies to term—would now serve as preparation, training, a prelude, an appetizer for the tribulations ahead. She would include on that list of ordeals the complete pain in the ass of navigating around Grand Junction, which uses fractions in street and road names—B 4/10 Road, for example, and 26 1/2 Road—a vexing system that cost Jason and Wendy a few minutes as they tried to locate the hospital. But they did find it.

Upon entering the waiting room, they were greeted by around twenty police officers and sheriff's deputies from Colorado and Utah who were there simply to show support for Wendy and solidarity for me. She was grateful for their presence and, at the same time, made more anxious by it. Cops came together to honor fallen officers—but I was still clinging to life! In an irrational part of her brain, it seemed like their mass presence in the waiting room might somehow put a thumb on the scale and turn into a self-fulfilling prophecy.

Chapter 10

"GOD, LIFE FORCE, ENERGY, KARMA"

The helipad at St. Mary's is on the roof of the fourteen-story building. Dr. Eric Hanly, the general trauma surgeon on call the night I arrived, instructed staff to wheel me directly to the operating room.

That ruffled a few feathers at the hospital. Normally, a patient arriving by helicopter would be taken first to the emergency room for assessment, then sent to the OR if necessary. Here was this new guy—Hanly had only been at St. Mary's for six months—disregarding the protocol. But it was absolutely the right call. Hanly knew I'd been shot. He'd seen X-rays from Moab's ER and talked to staff there about how much blood they'd pushed into me. "It was clear to me," he recalls, "this was somebody who was absolutely going to need surgery, right away."

I didn't actually meet him for another month, most of which time I spent in a medically induced coma. When we did finally talk (actually, I was still rasping after three and a half weeks with a ventilator down my throat), I learned that he and Wendy and I were kindred spirits: all of us had worked as river guides and had chosen to live in this part of the country to be closer to the Colorado.

Hanly grew up in Laramie, Wyoming, and went to college there. His father, a professor of violin and chamber orchestra at the University of Wyoming, was a former surfer from Western Australia. The professor liked Laramie but missed moving water. So he purchased a raft from a Sears & Roebuck catalog and set out exploring. When Eric was three, his father took him on a float trip down the Upper North Platte River through Saratoga, Wyoming, "and I was hooked," recalls the doctor, who was guiding trips by the time he was eighteen.

Hanly earned an Air Force scholarship that paid for his four years at Johns Hopkins University medical school. After five years in the Air Force working off that debt, he completed a one-year residency at Johns Hopkins, followed by a one-year fellowship at Duke University Hospital.

In the six months since he'd arrived at St. Mary's, Hanly hadn't treated a single gunshot victim. Would this be a problem for me? It would not. As part of his training, Hanly had spent four years treating a steady stream of gunshot victims, the grim consequence of endemic violent crime in Baltimore. As a result of that, he says, "I got really good at trauma surgery." He'd also spent the year at Duke as one of the hospital's critical care surgeons. "So I had done a lot of trauma leading up to this," he recalls, referring to my case. "I would say that I was at my absolute best."

Doctors later told me I'd "stabilized" during the helicopter ride. Asked if I was stable on the operating table, Hanly replies, "Well, stable's a relative thing. We're transfusing him blood continuously; he'd be dead without the blood, so that's not really stable." (They pushed another five units into me at St. Mary's for a total of twenty-one bags of blood in eight hours. A guy my size probably has around eleven or twelve units in him.) "But compared to somebody who's getting chest compressions because they have no blood pressure—compared to that, he was stable." Hanly continues, "The amazing thing is that he survived long enough to get to St. Mary's. Once he got to us, everything he had was something we could take care of."

But they still had to take care of it. Before being interviewed for this book, Hanly dug up his fourteen-year-old "operative file" from that night and early morning. Reading from the note, he mentions working that night with cosurgeon Sara Pereira, a cardiothoracic specialist. She focused on the organs in my chest while Dr. Hanly handled the wounds in my abdomen.

There are no surprises in Hanly's "preoperative diagnosis," which detected "multiple gunshot wounds to the abdomen, back and upper extremities." His "postoperative diagnosis" lists ten items:

- Multiple gunshot wounds to the abdomen, chest, back, and upper extremities
- Small bowel injuries, times eight
- Colon injuries, times four
- Right renal parenchyma contusion ("That's a kidney," Hanly explains.)
- Through-and-through gastric injury ("That's through-and-through the stomach," Hanly adds helpfully.)
- Through-and-through injury to the left lobe of the liver

- Diaphragm injury
- Left ventricle gunshot wound ("That's the left ventricle of the heart.")
- Open comminuted fracture of the left humerus ("Comminuted" in my case meaning "shattered into about twenty pieces.")
- Through-and-through gunshot wound of the right upper extremity

Hanly then produces another list, this one cataloging the procedures that were performed during the operation, which lasted "until five or six in the morning," he recalls. After ticking each of them off, he circles back to explain each step in more depth, using language more accessible to the layperson:

1. Exploratory laparotomy for trauma.
   "That just means 'Open the abdomen to explore and find out what the heck is going on.' When I examined him, as he was coming down the elevator, I could see in one of the gunshot wounds what's called omentum, which is a piece of fat that hangs off the transverse colon. We call it the watchdog of the colon, because when something goes wrong in the belly, omentum sticks itself to the problem, trying to contain it. One of the things we understand from our training: when you see that—omentum—it's an immediate 'Open the abdomen and find out what the problem is.'" Between that laparotomy and the sternotomy performed by Dr. Pereira, "We opened him up from just above his pubic bone to lower neck."

"GOD, LIFE FORCE, ENERGY, KARMA"

2. Small bowel resection with primary reanastomosis.

    "That means he had eight different holes in his small intestine. Fortunately, they were kind of clustered in one area, so I was able to remove all those holes in one segment of small intestine. You've got twelve to fifteen feet of small intestine. My recollection is that we took out two or three feet. Primary reanastomosis means reconnecting the ends."

3. Segmental colon resection with primary reanastomosis.

    "He had a similar thing on the right side of his colon. One of the bullets went through the colon wall in four different places: in, out, in, out. They were in the same general area, so I was able to get all four holes in one segment of colon, remove that, and then put the two ends back together. The colon is about five or six feet long, and we took about a foot."

4. Repair of liver laceration with application of energy and hemostatic agents.

    "One of the bullets went through his liver. We have these energy devices, electrocautery the most basic of them, that [allow doctors] to grab the bleeding vessels and just burn the end. Hemostatic agents have clotting factors, in powders or on a pad. We take those and put them on things that are bleeding to get them to stop."

5. Repair of missile gastrotomy.

    "It's a little dramatic, but we sometimes refer to bullets as missiles. That's all that means. Doesn't mean the perp had a rocket launcher. One of the bullets went through both the front and back walls of the stomach, so I had to repair both those holes."

6. Exploration of right perinephric hematoma with application of cautery for hemostasis.

   "We were seeing blood welling up from the back of the abdomen. And so we'll do these maneuvers to move the intestines out of the way so we can explore in that space, which is called the retroperitoneum. In this case, his was filling with blood from bleeding in the right kidney. So I had to go in and repair that and get that bleeding stopped."

7. Repair of diaphragm injury.

   "One of the bullets had traversed his diaphragm. So he had a hole in his diaphragm I had to repair."

8. Upper endoscopy to assess for esophageal injury.

   "We were worried about esophageal injury as well. Initially, he had blood coming from the tube [inserted in his nose] that was in his stomach. And when you see that, and it's obvious that he's had a bullet that's traversed part of the chest, you're worried about esophageal injury. So we did a scope down his esophagus to make sure it's not injured. In his case it wasn't. The blood was coming from holes in the stomach."

9. Washout of left humerus fracture; 10. Application of splint to left humerus fracture; 11. Washout of right upper extremity wound; 12. Washout of right groin wound; 13. Washout of right hip wound; 14. Washout of right flank wound; 15. Washout of right back wound.

"I don't do a lot of orthopedics, typically. In a case like this, you're not really all that worried about the fractures, in the moment. That's stuff you're doing later. But I did wash out that ['comminuted' left humerus] fracture so it wouldn't get infected and put a splint on it. And then washed out all those other wounds."

What about the bullet that grazed my heart? "It just basically nicked his ventricle," Hanly remembers. "Crazy, really. I remember Sara and I looking at it and thinking, 'Wow! I can't believe this guy's alive.'"

When a trauma laparotomy is performed—when they laid open my entire abdomen—Hanly explains, "We can do this thing called the subxiphoid pericardial window, where we sneak underneath the breastbone from within the abdomen and go into the pericardium," the sac around the heart. "So I did that and found blood in the pericardium, which is never a good thing, because it tells you definitively there's some sort of injury to the heart." Fortunately, in this case, it was just a "graze wound" to the ventricle, requiring only "a couple little stitches."

I got incredibly good care that night and morning. I was also incredibly lucky. "If any one of those bullets move[d] half an inch to the right, or left," Hanly marvels, I wouldn't have survived the night. "Like the bullet that went through the stomach. The fact that it didn't hit the aorta or the inferior vena cava"—a thin-walled blood vessel with the largest diameter in the venous system—"is amazing."

So how did I make it? How did I cheat death that night and in the days that followed? List maker that he is, Hanly enumerates three reasons. "Number one, he's a young healthy guy. He's got good tissues," says the doctor, referring to the thirty-four-year-old version of me (rather than my current, pushing-fifty self). "Two is God, life force, energy, karma—whatever you want to call it. It was all on his side." Well, it was certainly on my side before, during, and after the other guy ran out of bullets and stopped shooting me. "And three, things went well technically"—his understated way of saying that he and Dr. Pereira and anesthesiologist Steve Jones and everyone in the OR that night simply crushed it. "I've always seen Brody as my best save ever, and that remains true fourteen years later."

A brilliant trauma surgeon, he's also kept his whitewater rafting skills sharp. Years ago he met a guy—Hanly calls him a "mentor"—who taught him the ins and outs of getting down Cataract Canyon in a motor rig. So that's become one of his favorite things to do in life. In the subculture of "Cat" river rats, Hanly reports, he's known as the surgeon who took care of Brody Young. "It gives me a little street cred on the boat ramp most people don't have," he says with a smile. "Which is pretty cool."

Chapter 11

NOT OUT OF THE WOODS

At St. Mary's, I had the easy job: just lay there unconscious and let machines breathe for me and pump blood, saline, and plasma into me while a bunch of really smart, skilled doctors and nurses went about saving my life.

Back in the waiting room, Jason, Janel, and Wendy were going a trifle stir-crazy, battling the sleep monster and trying not to dwell on the worst-case scenario. To turn down the stress and get their minds off my situation, they told stories of bad dates and proms and rafting trips long since passed. "They were the best two people you could ever have in the hospital waiting room," says Wendy. "Their job was to help me not freak out. There were times we were laughing our guts out." Which is good, because every couple of hours, a surgeon would emerge with news of some previously undiscovered bullet or injury. As Wendy remembers, "They'd come out and say, 'We found this.' 'We found this.' They kept finding new holes. It was like the bullets were pinballing around inside him." But the blow was always cushioned by the news that I was hanging in there, hanging on. The surgeons kept rooting around and repairing me, and I kept . . . not dying.

All that night and for several days, the song remained the same, with doctors giving Wendy variants of the same refrain:

"He's not out of the woods yet."

"We're not out of the woods yet."

Just before dawn, the doctors finished operating on me. They sewed me up and sent me to what would be my new home for the next twenty-five days, a room in the intensive care unit. Later that morning, Wendy got the green light to visit me there. She asked Jason to join her and delegated to him the job of snapping a few pictures of me—even though this had been forbidden by the hospital. But Wendy wanted a record of what I looked like in those early hours and days. Part of the reason, as she told Jason, was so they could "show Brody what he put us through. If he ever says it wasn't that bad, we'll have these to show him." She was trafficking in slightly dark humor, as Wendy will. Of course she knew I was going through some things myself. But she was also giving voice to her belief, her *conviction*, that I was going to pull through, even though the doctors were still cautioning that I was by no means—all together now—out of the woods.

Jason was down to snap some illicit pictures but warned Wendy that he probably wouldn't be allowed in my room because he wasn't a family member. And nurses did indeed attempt to bar his entry, but they proved no match for the strength of Wendy's will. "Oh, he's from my church; he's *got* to come in with me," she declared as they barged in together without waiting for an answer.

Wendy tells me that I was puffy—nurses used the word *edematous*, meaning very swollen—and "didn't look anything like" myself. She stood beside me and whispered a greeting. She wanted to place her hand on me, but I had so many tubes going in and coming out that it was difficult for her to find a place to put her hand. After about five minutes, she took her leave. "I wasn't going to hang out there with all those doctors watching me," she says.

She had a phone call to make. Baby Jag had spent the night in the waiting room in his carrier. Now it was time for Wendy to share the news with our two oldest back in Moab—six-year-old Stryder and his three-year-old sister Jayde—that Dad had been shot.

Wendy called Kenna, whom our kids adored and who'd dropped everything on no notice when Wendy sent an SOS the night before. Kenna and her husband, Danny, hustled over and were waiting for the kids when they woke up Saturday morning. When Kenna picked up, Wendy asked how the kids were doing. "BEST SLEEPOVER EVER!" came the shouted reply. Our friends Kathleen and Steve had arrived early that morning bearing donuts and chocolate milk. Wendy's call had interrupted a party in progress. Kenna put the kids on speaker, and Wendy drew them out on the fun they were having. Eventually, one of them asked, "How come you left?" "Well," Wendy replied, "that's what I'm about to tell you."

Now, a brief digression is in order to explain why my children seldom call me "Dad." When they were small and trying to get my attention, they would repeat "Dad," each time louder and with more urgency: "Dad!" "DAD!" When I still failed to acknowledge them, they would shout "BRODY!" and I would invariably snap out of it and give them my attention. To this day, they refer to me most frequently as "Brody," not "Dad." As Wendy often helpfully points out, "You totally blew that one."

"Well, Brody got shot last night," she began. They digested that for a few seconds. Stryder, who was older, did most of the talking.

"By a bad guy?" he asked.

"Yeah, there was a guy, he was having a bad day, and he shot Brody."

"Is he all right?"

"I don't know. He's in the hospital, and he's asleep right now. So you can't really talk to him."

"Oh. OK."

Then she dropped some good news on them. Wendy's dad, their grandfather Steve (a.k.a. "Poppa"), was driving down in his big black SUV to take them over to Grand Junction. That was another treat. The kids loved their grandparents, who spoiled them, and were excited by the prospect of riding up high in Poppa's rig. "When you get here," said Wendy, "we'll talk some more about what happened."

"Is Brody going to be OK?" asked Stryder, seeking reassurance.

"I don't know," Wendy replied. "But we'll all get together and see how it goes."

"OK."

"OK."

At the end of the call, Wendy says, "they were fine. It was like, 'Who knew that when your dad gets shot, you get a sleepover and donuts?'" But this was the very beginning. Both would end up battling fear and anxiety and, in Jayde's case, deep anger that someone did this to her father. They grappled with that trauma long after my physical wounds had healed.

In the waiting room, Wendy was approached by a succession of well-wishers seeking updates. She was frazzled and running on no sleep but shared what information she could, qualifying her meager reports by saying, "I wasn't there. You probably heard about it before I did."

Steve arrived with Jayde and Stryder, who were told that I was still "sleeping" and that it was too early to visit me in my room. Then they waited for Wendy's mother, Debbie, who was flying back from Florida. Debbie had cut short a visit with her oldest daughter, Shelley, booking a 6 a.m. flight out of Sarasota Bradenton International Airport the next morning. Usually that flight is "full of senior citizens," reports Debbie, at that time a spry and youthful fifty-eight. "So it takes forever to get everyone's luggage loaded."

Not on this morning, however. At 5:45, the pilot got on the intercom to announce that since the flight was full and everyone was seated, they would be departing fifteen minutes early. Debbie's connecting flight out of Atlanta also left early. Upon arriving in Salt Lake, her suitcase—cue the heavenly chorus—was the first to appear on the baggage carousel, even though she has no status with Delta Airlines. We've joked that Debbie's suitcase might be the clearest evidence—aside from me not dying—that some divine hand was at work on our behalf. While that line always gets a few laughs in our family, I don't think any of us doubt that God had quite a bit to do with my survival. I can't prove that and don't intend to try. I do know what doctors have told me: I was hit by nine bullets, and six of those wounds could have—should have—been fatal on their own.

How is the guy still alive? The question on my mind isn't *why* I believe I was protected by my Maker. The question is, *How could I not?* While I hovered in that netherworld between life and death, members of my family drew great comfort from their faith and also a firm belief that this story would have a happy ending, even if it took years to get there.

Debbie got a lift from Salt Lake City to Grand Junction from her daughter Stephanie, Wendy's younger sister, who had just finished doing the dishes the night before when her dad called. Stephanie's husband, Dave, watched the color drain from her face during the call. "What's wrong?" he asked when she hung up. "Brody's been shot. They don't know if he's going to make it."

As the middle two of Steve and Debbie's four daughters, Stephanie and Wendy had always been tight—"partners in crime," as Steph puts it. Now she felt unmoored, as if "standing outside my body." Upon learning I was wounded, she and Dave and their young children went into the family room and knelt. Stephanie started the prayer, and within seconds, she remembers, "I had the most amazing feeling of peace. The tears stopped, and the panic was gone. It was like a blanket had been wrapped around me. I knew that everything was going to be OK."

Similarly, Wendy has spoken of the sense of well-being that came upon her during the two-minute drive from our house to Allen Memorial Hospital. Following her "two-second freak-out," as she described it, a calm came over her, an assurance that I was going to make it, and it never deserted her, even when she first saw me on the gurney, battling for each breath.

Her constant composure rippled out in concentric circles, sending the message to children and family and friends, *If Wendy is this confident that things are going to work out, that everything's going to be OK, then I can be too.* "That's how Wendy rolls," says her aunt Tammy Neslen. "She's kind of quiet, not an emotional wreck, and very strong. Her strength is unbelievable. She carried us all through this and made us stronger."

But on this night, coming up on forty hours without sleep, Wonder Woman's strength was waning. When the time came, she was happy to bail on that waiting room. "I was done being at the hospital," she remembers. But the hospital wasn't done with her.

She sent the following "Wendygram" to extended family on November 25, 2010:

NINE MIRACLES

Hi Everyone—

We just wanted to thank all of you for your love and support. This past weekend was a bit more exciting than planned. Instead of heading to Salt Lake for Thanksgiving we decided on Grand Junction. I am sure all of you know Brody was shot on Friday night while working. Thank goodness for the tender mercies of Heavenly Father and the quick response of the officers and ambulance or Brody would not be alive. The medical team at Allen Memorial was amazing in their response and quick action. They took an empty man & filled him up, corked up all the holes & readied him for his first helicopter ride. (Brody has been dying to ride on one!) I am so grateful for them.

He went through 7 hours of surgery Friday night. The surgeons were amazed at his injuries & his will to hang on. They were able to repair the damage to his intestines, colon, stomach, liver, kidney, diaphragm, heart & stabilized his arm.

Now we are just playing the waiting game. He has so many serious injuries & they still have to put his arm back together. He has had his moments—but is doing amazing considering all he has gone through.

The kids are doing great—they think we are on vacation over here. They are loving all of the attention from their aunts & grandparents. Stryder told me today that it seems like daddy is just out of town on one of his work trips. I kind of feel the same. At night when I get ready for bed I think I hope Brody will call me before 10 p.m. to say goodnight.

We just want all of you to know how much we appreciate all of the emails, text messages, phone calls, prayers, etc. We have the most amazing family & friends.

Thank you again for everything—You all are FANTASTIC!!

Love—Wen

Back in Bradenton, Shelley had booked two suites at the Marriott a couple miles east of town, out by the airport. Debbie, Steve, and Stephanie crashed in one. Wendy and our three kids took the other. Shelley burned through a small fortune in Marriott points to pick up the tab for those rooms. Once the hotel's management found out why Wendy and the kids were in town, Shelley was informed that her room would be comped. Ranking high among the countless acts of kindness and generosity raining down on us were those extended by staff members at that Marriott, who outdid themselves finding ways to lighten everyone's burden. Like the fictional Eloise at the Plaza Hotel in Manhattan, Stryder and Jayde had the run of the place. They had a blast frolicking in the hotel pool, which was made available to them any hour of the day or night. The doting man who ran the restaurant told them to order whatever they wanted, and it would be brought to them.

Lodging at the same hotel were many of the television and print journalists in town to cover the story of my shooting, which made national news. While Wendy appreciated the intense concern and interest and understood why the reporters and TV trucks were there, she declined interview requests. Her focus was on safeguarding our kids, creating a cocoon to shield them from the grim details of what had happened to me.

Two days after I was ambushed, she was working out in the Marriott fitness center near the hospital. It is understood by all who know her that Wendy's mood can be boosted by movement, some kind of workout. This is the woman who was going for jogs up until *the day before* Jag was born. Her doctors no longer told her not to run. They'd given up. At one point in her third trimester, they'd recommended bed rest. Instead, Wendy ran a 5K. And won her age group! Wendy was elated. The doctors, not so much.

During that Marriott workout, she had the bill of her ball cap pulled down to avoid being recognized. Reality rudely intruded, as it will, when a news channel aired a segment on the shooting and the manhunt in progress: "I was running on the treadmill, stressed out of my mind," Wendy remembers. "It was the first night I'd slept after he'd been shot, and I was hoping, *Please, don't let anyone be in here.* Of course they're showing what happened in Moab on the TV. There's Brody's truck, and there's this huge puddle of blood." After passing out but before I began rolling those thirty-five feet to the driver's side door, I lay in the dirt of the parking lot for I'm not sure how long. No more than five minutes. That was enough time for me to turn that patch of gravel a dark maroon—a palimpsest for the CSI folks to analyze and photograph and for the TV cameras to linger on, to Wendy's increasing ire.

We've worked with many journalists we like and respect, and we understand that "the media" is not a monolith, that outlets and standards vary widely. But as the days and weeks went by, Wendy and other family members had some general beefs about the coverage, which, in their eyes, dwelled more than necessary on the bloodshed. (And, yes, I was aware, as I typed that sentence, that a reader of this book might accuse me of the same thing—see the preceding paragraph.)

Some outlets reported that I'd been shot in the head, which, as Wendy noted, "was the one place he *didn't* get shot." Early reports also described my injuries as non-life-threatening—which, had I not been in a coma following seven hours of lifesaving surgery, would've been news to me. Other times, Wendy recollects, TV talking heads would say things that made her think, "How could they know that? I'm his wife, I'm in the hospital every day, and *I* don't know that. That part was really frustrating."

Frustrating for her at the time. Not so much for me.

Any guesses as to where I was at this time? I was in the pharmaceutically enhanced cloud of that coma and still in the woods, which is to say, not out of the woods. Not even close.

Chapter 12

HERE COMES DEBRIDE

I'd been running a slight fever following my surgery, which was to be expected. But that spiked up to 103 degrees on Sunday, accompanied by a return of my tachycardia, the racing heartbeat. My ticker was jackrabbiting along at 170 to 180 beats per minute—more than triple my resting pulse. Doctors tried a few intravenously infused drugs to bring that down, with limited success. The decision was made to bring in a heart surgeon who would perform—I'm reading from my own medical records here—an "ablation of the bypass tract via transseptal puncture," meaning the doctor would feed a catheter through a tiny surgical passage in a septum (wall) in my heart, then burn a predetermined group of cells in the left ventricle. That burn, or ablation, creates scarring that turns away the electrical signals causing the galloping heartbeat.

That procedure would be performed by Dr. Maria Anderson, but she would have to take a number. Four days after my seven-hour surgery, I went under the knife again. This time, Dr. Mary Beth Deering, an orthopedic surgeon, put my left arm back together by inserting a rod to hold the shattered humerus in place or, as it says in my medical record, "intramedullary nailing of the left humerus using a [DePuy] Synthes 7 × 290 mm. humeral nail (debridement and irrigation of L forearm, 2 bullet holes, bullet fragments, wash out bone fragments)." The doctor's note adds that she chose to "not remove other bullets not in easy proximity," as that "would disrupt soft tissue."

What is "debridement and irrigation"? Irrigation, in this context, is when a liquid solution is poured over an open wound to make it easier for the doctors and nurses to see. It also helps rinse debris from deeper parts of the wound. Debridement is the removal of infected tissue to promote healing.

Now, allow me to excerpt the next passage from my records, which should be titled "Here comes debride." Dr. Deering proceeded with the following:

- "Debridement and irrigation of R hip down to the level of muscle."
- "Debridement and irrigation of R forearm down to the level of the muscle."
- "Debridement and irrigation of R scrotum, superficial down to the level of the fascia"—the key word here being "superficial." The party tent suffered a minor tear, as I mentioned earlier, but the guests were unharmed.

Next, the doctor applied wound vacuum devices to my injured hip, right forearm, and, umm, "beanbag," as it were. Wound vacs, as they're called, gently pull fluid from the wound over time, reducing swelling and helping clean the injury. From beneath the adhesive film sealing the wound, a drainage tube leads to a portable vacuum pump. I spent a lot of time tethered to wound vacuums and thought of them as my friends. My brother-in-law, David Nordquist, Stephanie's hubby, had a different relationship with them. As we shall see.

It was so great to see Dave and Steph when they visited in December. Or rather, it would've been great if I hadn't been in that coma. I'm certain I picked up on their presence. For this visit, they were joined by Emma, their one-and-a-half-year-old daughter, and their feisty boxer, Hazel—"Z" for short. Debbie spotted them on the highway on their way into town. They were tough to miss, she noted. With the high chair, stroller, and kennel lashed to the roof of their Subaru wagon, they looked like the Joad family in *The Grapes of Wrath*.

During that visit, Dave was standing by my bedside, asking about the wound vacs. He says I was hooked up to seven of them that day. One of the nurses was explaining to him how they worked. She showed him the machine's "reservoir," which slowly filled with effluent pulled from the wounds. At that point, according to witnesses, Dave appeared to throw up a little in his mouth, then turned gray. "Wendy, I need to sit down," he said.

In those early weeks with me still comatose, Dave stood in for me as a surrogate pop (when the thought of wound vacs wasn't making him nauseous), roughhousing with the kids and reading to them from monster truck books he brought along. When I was in the ICU, baby Jag didn't want to be picked up by most people and wasn't bashful about letting them know. But he really liked being held by Rent-a-Dad Dave.

Basking in the attention of all those aunts, uncles, and grandparents, the kids actually had a blast, which, in turn, comforted the grown-ups. Stry and Jayde spent cheerful hours bowling in the corridors of the hospital. After rummaging through recycling bins for water bottles, they used those bottles as bowling pins, with a full water bottle serving as the bowling ball.

But the games came to an end, and our children could only be distracted for so long. I think Wendy's most herculean feat during those disruptive weeks was creating a routine for herself and the kids—imposing at least some semblance of structure on a fluid, unpredictable, and scary situation. "I had three kids that needed me to function like a regular mom," she remembers. "I needed *me* to function like a regular mom." Part of her routine became regular runs around Grand Junction. To get the kids—and herself—out of the Marriott, Wendy would somehow arrange all three of them on her state-of-the-art, stridently orange (ergo easily spotted by motorists) dual jogging stroller, a conveyance called the Bob.

Her favorite loop included a stiff climb made doubly difficult by the fact that she was pushing one-hundred-plus pounds of children. Near the summit of that hill, Wendy recollects, she always huffed past a group of landscapers who stopped what they were doing to watch her. Wendy would smile through her anaerobic grimace and say hello. The guys would wave and smile back. "Every time they saw me," she suspects, "they'd say, 'Here comes the crazy lady.'"

Pushing the Bob uphill, she evoked Sisyphus, the Greek mythological figure doomed to forever push a boulder up a hill, only to have it roll back down as he neared the summit. But Wendy was more stubborn than Sisyphus and eventually reached the top. It took a while, but she got there. And then things got easier. Alas, she wasn't—we weren't—even close to the summit.

The following is her Wendygram from December 6, 2010:

> Sorry the updates have been a little slow. This past week has been Mr. T tough! Just when we thought everything was working its way out—Brod decided to pull some fast ones on us! (Just like him, right?!) So, if you recall, last Friday Brod had heart surgery to slow down his racing heart. It went really well. The surgery was a breeze! The doctors decided that he was doing so well that they could start weaning him from the ventilator. That started on Saturday. The first try didn't really go—Brod freaked out. So they decided to hold off until later . . .
>
> Anywho—his temp has stayed up all week & the ventilator has stayed in . . . meaning my kids still have not seen their dad. This week has been extremely rough on them. Hopefully next week will be the one! Jayde has

been so homesick for Brod that she just cries & cries every night. Her most awesome nursery teacher sent us a picture of our family [snapped at church just days before the ambush] & we hung it right next to her face on the wall near her bed. It has been a lifesaver. She falls asleep looking at our number 5 family all smiling at her! We have been saying special prayers at night for each of the kids at bedtime as well. The other night Jayde was so sad & I asked if she wanted a special prayer. She said yes, but she wanted the one where daddy puts his hands on her head. A good hint that maybe all of us needed some extra help! . . .

On Wednesday, the doctors decided to put Brody back on the ventilator 100%. He has been extremely agitated and anxious all week. His fever has remained a constant as well. They decided to do another chest X-ray. The X-ray did not look as good as they hoped. There appeared to be a bunch of fluid hanging out in places it shouldn't. They did another CAT scan to see if maybe some fluids from his gut had come to vacation in the lungs. Things still looked a bit awry. They did discover another bullet though. Pretty amazing since he has had at least 3 other CAT scans already. This new bullet is in the L2 region of the spine. More details on that once I speak with the neurosurgeon . . .

Overall, we are doing well. It has just been a bit of a week . . .

Grand Junction may be the most confusing place on this earth—street wise, but they sure know how to make parks. The kids & I have spent many fun hours playing on the playgrounds, riding scooters & the boot scoot. Our new favorite activity is feeding the ducks at the park. You see, the pond is frozen & the ducks run & slide on the ice for bread & crackers. They crash & spin & do all sorts of tricks. It's like our own little hockey game in pursuit of bread! Thank heavens for the ducks!

Thanks again for everything. Please remember that this is a positive experience. Brod is doing well. He is a miracle! He is getting better slowly but surely. Please do not be worried or sad. We are being taken care of by the best caretaker there is!

Wen

FYI—please hold off on coming to visit Brod. He is extremely sick right now. If he gets a cold, cough or the flu, we will lose tons of hard-fought ground. The docs have asked that only immediate family visit right now. I only go in 2 times a day. He is very heavily sedated & rarely knows when I go in. Once he is doing better, we are planning on setting up Skype sessions so he can visit everyone over the internet. We will keep you posted. Thanks for your understanding.

Pontiac Grand Am found deserted the morning after Brody was ambushed. Photo taken November 20, 2010.

Lance Arellano's last known location, where he deserted a backpack, rifle, and supplies. Photo taken November 20, 2010.

Lance's backpack, coat, torn shirt sleeve, and rifle. These items were deserted at Lance's last known location.

Lance's shirt, deserted at his last known location. The sleeve was cut off and possibly used as a tourniquet. Photo taken November 20, 2010.

Lieutenant Tony White teaching rangers at
The Farm range during the spring of 2009.

Brody's truck, November 19, 2010, view of open driver's side door.

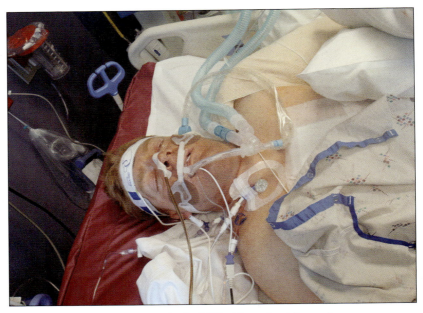

Brody in a coma in the ICU with twelve tubes going in and ten coming out, November 2010.

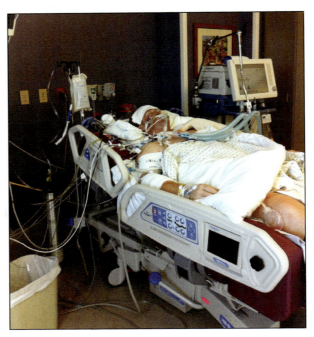

Brody comatose in St. Mary's Hospital, November 2010.

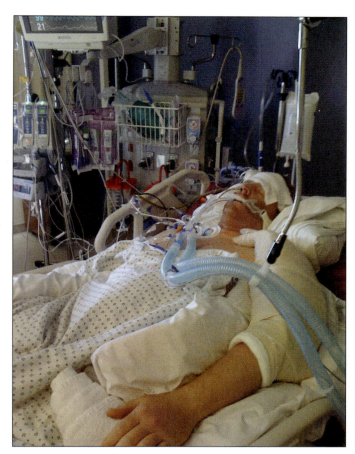

Brody comatose in St. Mary's Hospital, November 2010.

Overview of Brody's patrol truck at Poison Spider Mesa trailhead.

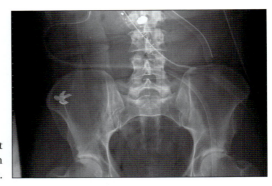

Brody's X-ray of the bullet lodged in his hip and in the vertebrae in his back.

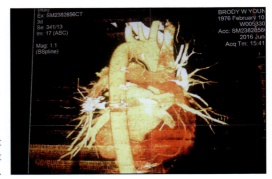

3D image of Brody's heart with a bullet next to his left ventricle by the esophagus.

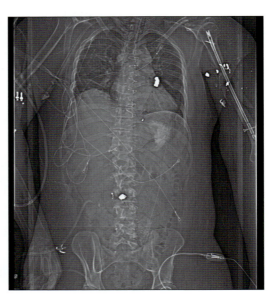

X-ray of Brody's chest and spine.

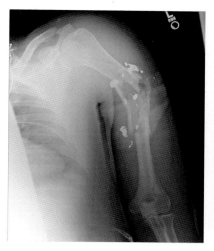

X-ray of Brody's left humerus, with no rod and scattered bullet shrapnel.

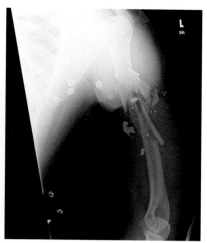

X-ray of Brody's left humerus, straightened before surgery.

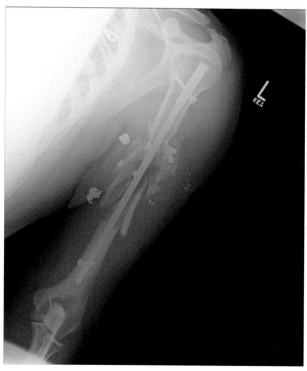

X-ray of Brody's left humerus, with a rod in place.

The Young family, 2012.

Brody's website information.

The Young family on the shore, 2012.

CHAPTER 13

ANGELS APPEAR

One day in the waiting room, Wendy noticed a smallish sixty-something man seated nearby with a hacking cough attributable, she later learned, to his hardcore smoking habit. Eventually, after working up his courage, the man approached Wendy and said, with an air of apology, "I know you have people coming up to you all the time. But I have an offer I hope you'll consider." His name was Lee Searcy, and he served as a reminder, like Clarence Odbody in *It's a Wonderful Life*, that angels come in unexpected forms.

Lee owns an assisted living facility for elderly people. "I have a house for you to live in," he said. "It's across the street, a block down." The house was in a gated community, which appealed to Wendy, who'd grown weary of the reporters hanging out around the hospital. "Just come over and see it," Lee implored. To humor him, she did.

The house was beautiful—not that big, but bigger than our home in Moab. Wendy felt obligated to point out that our children could be rambunctious and, at times, very loud, which surely would pose a problem at an assisted living facility. "Not at all," countered Lee, who pointed out that the closest neighbor was a delightful woman who also happened to be quite deaf. Wendy thanked Lee for his thoughtfulness, then broke the news that we couldn't afford to pay him anything. We were suddenly down two incomes, and we weren't exactly flush before that. "I don't need any money," said Lee.

Wendy relented, and they moved to the Hilltop assisted living community. Lee arranged for employees to furnish the place with beds, couches, and a big-screen TV. On move-in day, he handed Wendy a fat stack of vouchers for the cafeteria, saying, "We have chefs that will cook whatever you want."

Now, some chose to interpret Arellano's ambush of me as further proof of the entropic, irreversible, downward spiral of humankind. Wendy recalls someone lamenting, "This just opens up your eyes to how horrible the world is." We believe that person got it exactly wrong. Lance's solitary action, it turned out, opened a floodgate of charity, generosity, thoughtfulness, and love. "All these people used it as an opportunity to be amazing and help us out in ways we couldn't have foreseen," says Wendy, still incredulous fourteen years later. "That's the thing that blew my mind."

Lee was one of four people who offered Wendy and the kids their homes to live in. Others offered their cars. Perfect strangers sent money, "which was huge," Wendy remembers, because even before I got shot, we were living pretty close to the bone after paying the mortgage and utilities. Now we would have some hospital bills on top of that. People we knew and many, many more we'd never met donated to fundraisers and directly to us—each gift a humbling reminder that most people are intrinsically good.

Every church in Grand Junction—and there are a *lot* of churches in this town—offered prayers for me and for our family. A local healing center held a special event, scheduled to coincide with the full moon, to harness that powerful lunar mojo and channel it in my direction. A group of orange-robed Tibetan monks who heard about the shooting and happened to be in town swung by the hospital. They weren't offended that they couldn't get into the ICU to see me. I mean, they're monks. But they still chanted some healing mantras for me. I know it helped.

Arellano's act of evil ended up illuminating this truth: there's far more good in the world than the bad that tends to be amplified on the news. As Wendy put it, "My faith in humanity blew through the roof."

Wendy visited the hospital in the morning and in the evening, with the middle of her day devoted to the kids. The baby was still nursing. Jayde was a precocious three, but she was still three. They needed constant attention, and Wendy gave it to them. She homeschooled Stryder and got the kids out quite frequently.

Their new casa and the surrounding homes were pristine and immaculate, "not a blade of grass out of place," Wendy remembers. Not for long. Living a couple hours and one state away, our kids missed their pals. So their parents would drive them over en masse. It was an amazing sacrifice on the parents' part and a lifeline for Wendy. On a given afternoon, there might be a half dozen or eight boisterous, shrieking children marauding around the assisted living community like a band of miniature Visigoths, trampling gardens and riding bikes and scooters on lawns.

Stephanie and Dave had brought down a big packet of sidewalk chalk, which proved a great hit with our young visitors. They would take turns lying on the sidewalk, sprawled as if pushed from a skyscraper. While the "victim" lay still, others made a chalk outline of the body. Slightly morbid though it was—especially considering why they were in Grand Junction in the first place—those art projects proved a popular diversion. Octogenarians out on their daily constitutionals soon became accustomed to the sight of body outlines.

Lee Searcy, the saintly chain-smoker, would smile like the Buddha at reports of the trodden-upon front yards and chalk depredations, then ask Wendy if there was anything else he could do for her. We are endlessly grateful to him and to the parents who made the sacrifice of hauling their children to another state so that Stryder and Jayde could forget for a few hours that Dad could still not speak to them.

Some sacrifices were greater than others, as our friend Jason Taylor likes to remind us. After pulling into Grand Junction late one morning, his wife, Jen, asked Wendy what she felt like doing. Her surprising response, because Wendy is very health conscious, was that she wanted to go to McDonald's and unleash the kids on its vast PlayPlace.

Jason flinched. He'd made a New Year's resolution fifteen years earlier to never return to the Golden Arches.

ANGELS APPEAR

Driving to Vegas in 1995, he and a couple buddies got some bad beef in their Quarter Pounders, they believe. Navigating the narrow, twisting road through Virgin River Gorge, each was afflicted with chronic and voluminous diarrhea, requiring them to pull over frequently. "We were hanging off the side of the road, doing our business," Jason remembers, "and I vowed never to eat McDonald's again. That was my New Year's resolution." It was a pact he'd honored until that afternoon in Grand Junction. When Wendy mentioned the Playland, Jason was about to bring up the subject of his ironclad resolution when his wife, with steel in her voice, informed him, "You're *going* to McDonald's, you're going to eat there, and you're going to enjoy it."

Most days, in that eventful first fortnight after having my arms, butt, and torso ventilated free of charge, there was some fresh piece of bad news, such as when my heart decided to start racing again or when the doctors found a previously undiscovered "missile." But the bearers of bad news were not restricted to medical personnel.

In early December, Wen got a call from the principal of the elementary school where Stryder was a first grader. Basically, she was calling Wendy to inform her that Stryder was being expelled. "He hasn't been coming to school," the woman told her, "and we haven't gotten any notes from you." "Yeah," replied Wendy, not quite able to disguise her incredulity, "we've had this other thing going on with my husband being shot nine times." The principal agreed that it was awful, my being wounded and having to fight for my life. But this did not change the fact that Stryder's absences were unexcused. And now that he'd missed too much class to make up, he would have to be unenrolled. She suggested Wendy find a new elementary school in Grand Junction and send him there.

That's when another angel alighted in our lives.

While I'm chilling in my coma at this point in the narrative, please indulge a brief theological digression, which will help explain why we felt so supported during those tough, scary months. Catholic friends have told me about their parishes—defined communities entrusted to a pastor, who preaches and instructs parishioners in the faith. Our church's rough equivalent is called a ward. Wards are arranged using defined geographic borders. There's no ward shopping. You go to the meetinghouse in your assigned area. That's by design. Unlike most American Christians, as the *Atlantic* writer McKay Coppins explained in a 2021 essay, Latter-day Saints don't choose whom they go to church with: "They're assigned to congregations based on geographic boundaries often gerrymandered to promote socioeconomic diversity. And because the Church is run almost entirely by volunteers, and every member is given a job, they have to work together closely."

It's true that it would take some pretty creative gerrymandering to find much diversity in Moab. But this is also true: that enforced community has blessed us with some of the most meaningful relationships in our lives. Yeah, it can be a bit messy. We're all human. "Our little community wasn't perfect," as Coppins wrote of his diverse congregation in the Brooklyn neighborhood of Bushwick. "We argued and irritated one another. . . . But the dynamic was better than utopian—it was hard. Over time, we learned to live a portion of our lives together, to 'mourn with those that mourn,' as the Book of Mormon teaches, 'and comfort those that stand in need of comfort.'"

Yes, Utah is a deeply conservative state—but that conservatism differs from the ideology in vogue in other deep-red states. It's cut with more tolerance and compassion. The anti-immigrant rhetoric that's a staple of Republican politics elsewhere gets far less traction in Utah, in part, writes Coppins, "because the stories of pioneer suffering"—recall the "extermination order" signed by Missouri's governor in 1838—"have also instilled in many American Mormons a sensitivity to the experiences of immigrants and refugees."

Citing still another way Latter-day Saints go against the grain of conservative orthodoxy, Coppin notes that Utahans generally "don't romanticize rugged individualism or Darwinian hyper-capitalism." Members of the state's "tightly networked faith communities" abide by a shared moral obligation to lift up their brothers and sisters in time of need, "to comfort those that stand in need of comfort."

Which is where Jill Tatton comes in. We'd known and been friends with her before she became Stryder's first-grade teacher at Red Rock Elementary School. She and her husband were members of our ward. Jill was in her second year at Red Rock Elementary. She was one of those young teachers who practically vibrated with purpose and passion for her work. She was patient, energetic, an incandescent light. We knew we were lucky to have her. Until I got shot, we didn't know *how* lucky.

Stryder was our first child, so we were probably a little more enthusiastic about volunteering than we were, say, once we had three in school. Just bein' real. Wendy and I were in her classroom pretty much weekly. One day I wore my park ranger uniform and talked to the kids about the job. Yes, I told the class, when the question was posed, I do carry a gun when I'm working. No, I replied to the inevitable follow-up, I've never had to use it.

Then came the night that changed, and Wendy had to pull Stryder out of school for six weeks to be with his family in Grand Junction. That's when Jill showed us who she really was. On top of teaching every day, she would make the 220-mile round trip to and from Grand Junction once or twice a week. She brought homework assignments, lesson plans, and cards and posters from Stry's classmates telling him how much they missed him. Her students also made incredibly cute "get well" cards, which awaited me when I rejoined the sentient world.

I never realized, until I talked to Jill a few years later, how deeply shaken she was when I was injured and how extremely worried she'd been about Wendy and all three kids. During her weekly drive to St. Mary's, as she dropped down toward Grand Junction on I-70, the vast plateau of the Colorado National Monument looming on her right, Jill would feel her anxiety building. It was her job, as she saw it, to project calm and strength and confidence that all would be well. But the closer she got, the more she felt her emotions building. She was afraid, she recalls, that she would "just start bawling in front of the kids."

That didn't happen, Jill explains, "because Wendy was such a pillar of strength. She was so amazingly together. I wanted to be helping her, but she was helping me get through this whole thing." By the end of her visit, Jill remembers, "I would feel a peace, knowing that everything was going to be OK." Back in the classroom, Jill had to be a fact-checker at times, dismissing some of the myths racing around the school—that I'd been shot twenty times, for instance, or that I had died, or that I was in a coma from which I'd never emerge.

What Wendy and Jill ended up doing was unenrolling Stryder from Red Rock. Technically, he was homeschooled for the final month of that fall semester—that way the district's attendance policy didn't affect him. "But I kept him on the same curriculum," Jill recalls. She would bring books and assignments to Grand Junction. Wendy taught him during the day, made sure he did his homework, and administered tests. Jill did some teaching on her weekly visits, helping Stryder with material he wasn't grasping. I'm still not sure how she did it, but Jill made him feel not just involved in the class but like an important part of it. During a truly fraught time, she was a steadying presence, helping Wendy assure Stryder that I would recover, that we would all go home, and that life would be good again and normal.

But first, I'd have to emerge from my medically induced hibernation.

Chapter 14

THE "F" WORD

●

I remember two dreams from my twenty-four days in a medically induced coma. In one of them, I was still in my hospital bed, but the bed was in a train car traveling east. Standing all around were doctors, looking down at me, talking among themselves. Intermingled among them, despite their lack of proper scrubs and gloves, were my loved ones and family members, including my mother, who'd left us a decade earlier. Everything was bathed in golden light. I don't know the source of the light—maybe the Holy Spirit, or possibly a chandelier, for this was one of those fancy old-school club cars with upholstered chairs and wood paneling.

Thanksgiving was close, in both the dream and real life, and the train was taking us to Plymouth Rock, Massachusetts. We're all pilgrims on our individual journeys, but the pilgrimage, the journey, is enriched and made worthwhile by the fellowship of those we love. At least, that's how I'm interpreting the appearance of Plymouth Rock in this dream. Nobody on the train was scared or anxious or bringing any kind of negative energy. They were smiling, looking down at me, exuding a uniform certainty that every little thing, to borrow from Bob Marley, was going to be alright. It was profoundly comforting and reassuring. I was suffused with a feeling of safety and well-being, although that might have been the morphine talking.

The second vivid dream came later. This time around I was angry—convinced for reasons I could not tell you—that my fellow patients and I were being used, without our consent, as extras in a CSI show. I was thinking, *Ahh—this is how hospitals make their money.* So I kind of lost it and started yelling and pulling tubes out. I remember a nurse being angry with me—this wasn't part of the dream—restraining me and pointing a finger at me because I'd misbehaved. Then I was worried that they were going to kick me out. Then I was back in LaLa Land.

I'd been in that reversible coma for sixteen days or so when the docs and anesthesiologist decided it was time to start dialing back the drugs that kept me asleep. Call it Coma Lite. As luck would have it, on the first day I fully emerged from that drug-induced sleep, I was greeted by the sight of my stalwart friend Jason Taylor, who'd survived that tumble off the McDonald's wagon without a reprise of his epic gastrointestinal tumult. I wish I'd summoned some memorable remark, like "I come back to you now, at the turn of the tide," as Gandalf tells Aragorn in *The Lord of the Rings: The Two Towers.* Instead, I got mad at Jason because I was parched, thirstier than I'd ever been, and he wouldn't give me water.

When I pleaded for it—actually, I rasped unintelligibly, having not used my vocal cords in almost a month—he shrugged and said, palms facing upward, "Sorry, man." Jason didn't bring me water when I asked because he saw the tracheostomy tube coming out of my neck. To wean patients off the ventilator, they reduce the amount of oxygen it delivers, forcing us to work, to breathe once again on our own. I agree with that method in principle, but man, sometimes it felt like slow suffocation. "I don't know the ins and outs of a trach," Jason later explained. "There were no nurses around. If I give him a syringe of water, what if it goes right into his lungs, and he drowns on me? I can just see the headline: 'Man Survives Nine Bullets, Drowns on Three Ounces of Water.'"

The nurses finally did show up and made a fuss over me, but my request was denied. I just wanted a little taste of frickin' water. To appease my thirst, I was finally granted little paper cups of ice chips. I never want to forget how amazing it felt to experience even those simple things: Breathing and swallowing on my own. The sublime sensation of ice melting on my tongue, cooling my parched throat. The touch of my wife and children. The day finally came when I would get back on solid foods. I ordered salmon. A nurse's assistant brought me a piece of dry, overcooked hospital salmon. It was so good I almost wept.

The following is a Wendygram from December 13, 2010:

> Let's get to it! Last email I mentioned that Brod had been breathing on his own during the day. Well, he has been doing it around the clock since last Friday! The ventilator was officially removed from his room Saturday morning! He is still breathing through the trach,

enjoying the pure, unadulterated oxygen that only the hospital can provide, but he is breathing nonetheless! He has also become very awake and aware! He is no longer enjoying the high life . . . you could say. It is great to see the Birdman is back.

If you recall last week, Brod had to take a nap after brushing his teeth. Well now he spends at least 4 hours a day sitting up in his recliner. That's got to feel good after 3 weeks in a hospital bed. The nurse told me today that he even stood up & shuffled a few steps—baby steps, of course. I told Brod today that the race is on between Jag and him to see who will walk first.

Both Stry & Jayde have been in to see Brod in his new coherent state. It sure made them happy. Jayde did not want to leave Brod when it was time to go. We actually exited ICU with Jayde over my shoulder yelling, "You can't keep my daddy here!" We are hoping that for our next visit, Brod will be able to talk.

We are hoping Brod will graduate from ICU by the end of the week. His wounds are healing nicely—miracles in and of themselves! He is awake and alert & cruising like an old man with Parkinson's.

. . . We still have a long road ahead of us. The doctors said if all goes perfect, we will be home the end of January or mid-February. But we will be returning home together. What more could we ask?

Wen

THE "F" WORD

Next is a Wendygram from just six days later, December 19, 2010:

> Every day brings about more little miracles. Brod finally got to eat real food this weekend. They removed the feeding tube from his nose & he is in charge of getting his manly figure back.
>
> We are enjoying our visits with him. The kids are happier & have mellowed out now that daddy is no longer off limits. Jag enjoys the hospital bed—he can throw any number of things off and they make great noise hitting the floors! I even get to call Brod at night before bed. Tonight I actually heard a bit of his voice among the whispering. Good medicine for my soul . . . his too I hope!
>
> Tomorrow the investigation begins . . . so please keep Brod in your thoughts and prayers. He is pretty pumped about finally getting all the info out about what happened. Hopefully it will bring him peace of mind. The docs are giving the investigators one day to get their info, and then Brod starts intense post-traumatic stress therapy. (It's a good thing—he has been having terrible night terrors.) I am glad that he is finally going to start this other road of healing.

So much positive news in Wendy's terrific dispatches. Never one to avoid hard truths, she also touches on my post-traumatic stress, which manifested in night terrors, yes, but also plagued my waking hours.

So many good things were happening—small, simple acts as I mentioned, like breathing on my own again, and swallowing, and feeling the sublime sensation of ice melting on my tongue, cooling my throat.

However, this was also a dark time for me, a period of profound anxiety. Awaiting me, as I returned to waking life, were countless blessings—but also the news that the man who shot me hadn't been found and might still be at large.

Details of the attack returned in sharper focus the further I emerged from the coma. *I've been shot . . . Please help me . . .* I couldn't help but relive those moments: the shocking impact of the first bullet, the uselessness of my left arm, the muzzle flash of his gun, and his inexorable advance as I lay on the ground, absorbing one round after the next.

I don't think of myself as a hero. A hero probably wouldn't be as reliant as I am, every morning, on the snooze button. But a friend of mine has talked to me about the hero's journey, as outlined by the late Joseph Campbell, an author and teacher best known for his work in the field of comparative mythology.

Campbell's archetypal hero "ventures forth from the world of common day into a region of supernatural wonder," according to his book *The Hero with a Thousand Faces*. In my case, this friend points out, that "common day" world would be me standing at the kitchen counter bolting an early supper, then climbing into my truck to work that overtime shift. The "region of supernatural wonder" is the canyon on the far side of the Portal, the towering ocher cliffs and petroglyphs one passes on the way to the Poison Spider Mesa trailhead.

Campbell's hero wins a "decisive victory," then returns from that supreme ordeal with the "power to bestow boons" on his community. *Boon* is a dusty, archaic word for benefit or favor or gift.

What gift, what wisdom, did I bring back from my ordeal to share with others? I discovered the full power of forgiveness. I experienced its transformative, uplifting properties. The grace it brings.

Those flashbacks plaguing me in the hospital, along with the knowledge that Arellano remained at large—all that gnawed at me and preyed on my mind. I felt what Hunter S. Thompson might have recognized as fear and loathing of the world beyond the walls of my hospital room.

It was a pervasive dread and angst such as I'd never experienced. I mean, even when I wasn't on the river, I had always floated figuratively on the surface of things, never really letting anything get me too down for too long. I was the chill park ranger who prided himself on making people smile—even when I was citing them. Before that, I was a drummer, a clean hippie, and an ultimate Frisbee player. On my Missouri mission, I would smile in the face of rejection, for it is in opposition, I'd been taught, that we grow in strength and character.

But this postcoma darkness was getting the better of me, threatening to engulf me. I pleaded and prayed and begged for relief. And then one day, I had an epiphany, and the fever broke. It wasn't any kind of calculation on my part—it wasn't something I decided to do because I thought it would banish the scorpions from my head and give me peace, let me rest. It was more like a sudden gift of inspiration imparted from on high—like the apple bopping Isaac Newton on the head or the "tongues of fire" descending on the disciples in the book of Acts. I'd been obsessing about Arellano and the harm he did to me—and might still do to me or my family—and it was making me miserable. Then this imperative lodged itself in my brain: *Just forgive him.*

So I did.

I'd learned from investigators that Lance had a tough life, a rough go with an abusive stepdad, which helped explain his hostility toward anyone carrying a badge. Once I felt a flash of sympathy for him, it was easier to forgive him, to set my burden down, that cargo of dread, agitation, and vengeance.

It doesn't always work this way, but in my case, relief was pretty much immediate. My mind cleared like the sky after a storm. I felt a weight lifted, an opening inside. It freed up bandwidth somehow. Am I making sense? In setting down that burden, I'd created space to heal and experience joy and reclaim my life. All that sprung from an act of forgiveness.

That's not surprising. Forgiveness, I've learned, can have significant health benefits. That's my lived experience. It's also been proved by a host of studies. Acts of forgiveness can have huge rewards for your health, according to experts at Johns Hopkins Medicine: "lowering the risk of heart attack; improving cholesterol levels and sleep; and reducing pain, blood pressure, and levels of anxiety, depression and stress."

Those who cling stubbornly to grudges, on the other hand, "are more likely to experience severe depression and post-traumatic stress disorder, as well as other health conditions."

"Dwelling on wounds gives them power over you," writes Dr. Fred Luskin, the author of *Forgive for Good*. Luskin is a pioneer in the field of forgiveness research (yes, that's a thing) and the director and cofounder of the Stanford University Forgiveness Project. "When we think about a hurt," he writes, "our body reacts as if it is in danger and activates what is known as the fight-or-flight response." That response triggers the release of "stress chemicals" that prepare us to either fight back or run away: "They cause the heart to speed up and blood vessels to constrict. This raises blood pressure. Our liver dumps cholesterol into our bloodstream so that it can gum up our heart in case we lose too much blood. The stress chemicals alter our digestion and cause our muscles to tighten. Our breathing becomes shallower, and our senses are heightened to cope with the problem at hand. Digestion ceases, and blood flow is diverted to the center of the body. We feel jumpy and uncomfortable."

Those stress chemicals were valuable allies—lifesavers, probably—in my battle with Arellano. But they weren't doing me any favors in the weeks that followed, as I regained consciousness and started reliving those moments in my mind. Now I was just tormenting myself.

Chronic stress and anger take a physical toll on the body, according to numerous experts. It puts you into a fight-or-flight mode, resulting in numerous changes in heart rate, blood pressure, and immune response. Forgiveness, however, calms stress levels, leading to improved health. That was certainly my experience. By forgiving Arellano, I was taking power back from him. I was limiting the amount of space in my mind that I would rent to him, to borrow one of Luskin's metaphors.

Here's what I wasn't doing: I wasn't saying that I wanted to be his friend or that I'd forget what he did to me. Forgiveness isn't the same thing as absolution, notes Karen Swartz, MD, a specialist in mood disorders at the Johns Hopkins Hospital. "People get hung up on saying, 'If I forgive you, somehow I've forgotten, or you're not in trouble.' Forgiveness is something different, which is saying, 'I am not going to have these negative emotions consume me. I am going to move forward.'"

Nor is forgiveness a one-and-done phenomenon. You don't forgive someone, then simply forget the transgression and move on. As Luskin teaches, it's a skill you practice, a muscle you need to develop.

I still have pain—in my reconstructed left arm and patched-up abdomen, to name two places. There are others. I loved playing pickup basketball, just as I loved running the trails around this harsh, beautiful outback. But trail runs and pickup hoops are no longer in my repertoire, thanks to Lance. And I'm at peace with that—grateful for the activities still available to me. We live and adapt. There's this profound quote from Marcus Aurelius, the Roman emperor and Stoic philosopher, who observed that "the impediment to action advances action. What stands in the way becomes the way."

That's not to say I don't have some dark thoughts about him on occasion. But then I remind myself, "Hey, you forgave him. Let it go."

And I do. Because this is what I believe: Arellano and I are going to meet again. And our gunfight is going to be ancient history, water under the bridge. It's not even going to matter. He was going through a rough time, and I wandered into his crosshairs. It was nothing personal. That's not to say I didn't want to see him captured and tried in a court of law. I could forgive him all I wanted, but I wouldn't try to spare him the consequences of those actions. That's not my call. But catching him was out of my hands. I learned to be at peace with that.

Chapter 15

WAYBACK MACHINE

In the process of researching this book, I listened to a recording of radio traffic that night made by the Consolidated Dispatch Center in Price, Utah, which provides communications services to about three dozen state and local agencies across southeastern Utah.

Before climbing into the Wayback Machine to hear myself send out a desperate call for help, I want to express my gratitude and deep respect for dispatchers, who are highly trained, light on their feet, cool under pressure, and "patient but firm," as our own Jenny Swenson has written, with a sense of "when to take charge, but [who] also know when to just listen." Jenny is the dispatch supervisor at the Grand County Sheriff's Office and sang the praises of her tribe in a letter to the editor for the *Moab Sun News*. "Dispatchers never know what will be on the other end of the line," she wrote, "but they have to be ready to deal with anything."

As if to underscore her point, the recording from the night I was shot begins with an exchange between the Price dispatcher and a highway patrolman who is providing the precise location of a dead cow elk on the highway. (It was "on the fog line" at milepost 93.)

NINE MIRACLES

A few minutes later, a familiar voice says, "Two alpha six-nine, two alpha twenty." That's my supervisor, Tony White—whose call sign is two alpha twenty—trying to hail me on the radio. Hearing no reply, he repeats the call. The next voice is my own. Reliving that instant fourteen years later is chilling, surreal, and ultimately gratifying—I'm still here!

It is also a reminder that our memories can be malleable. Nowadays, when I deliver motivational speeches, I dwell on that moment in the parking lot when, having rolled those thirty-five feet to the truck and at last grasping the microphone, I compose my thoughts and speak coolly into it.

But it turns out that's not *exactly* how it went down. I mean, I wasn't panicked. But I wasn't calm either. I left no doubt that my situation was *dire*:

"Price two alpha six-nine [*Crackle of static, muffled verbiage*] . . . BEEN SHOT. I'm at Poison Spider. Please help me."

"Two alpha six-nine, copy. You've been shot on Poison Spider."

"YES—HELP!"

At that point, I let go of the microphone, lay down on my back, and started stringing breaths together. I did not make another radio transmission that night. But I could hear those blessed dispatchers—first in Price, then in Grand County—putting the word out. Now I just needed to hang on. Help was on the way.

The same week I heard that recording, I saw, for the first time, the full video from the dashboard of Al Cymbaluk, the sheriff's deputy whose concerned face appeared, hovering over me, nine minutes—*nine minutes!*—after I called in.

Cymbaluk was first on the scene that night, with Moab police officer Shaun Hansen. It's tense as they drive up to the parking lot, gravel crunching under their tires. Those guys had no idea what might be waiting for them. Even before he stops, Hansen is out of the car, walking ahead, rifle in hand, scanning the perimeter. He covers his partner while Cymbaluk tends to me. (That was really brave, guys. Thank you again.)

After passing along the information I had—a description of the suspect, his car, a partial plate number—I lapsed back into silence. It was getting so hard to draw a breath that I tried to sit up at one point. "I think you should lay flat," Cymbaluk tells me gently. While he asks me to "hold tight," Hansen trots back to their vehicle to give dispatch the make and model of the car and the partial license plate.

Dispatchers in Price sprung immediately into action—calling state police officers at home and phoning St. Mary's to get a helicopter in the air (at Tony White's request)—all while juggling an intense volume of radio traffic. From the outset, dispatchers coordinated with officers to get roadblocks and checkpoints set up that would prevent the shooter from escaping. Cars were soon being stopped at Crescent Junction, forty-two miles north of Moab, where the north-south artery of Highway 191 T-bones into I-70. Meanwhile, twenty miles south of Moab, San Juan County sheriff's deputies set up a checkpoint at La Sal Junction.

Other early responding law enforcement agents posted up near Moab Giants Dinosaur Park, eleven miles north of town. That's where Highway 191 intersects with Dead Horse Mesa Scenic Byway. That road, favored by tourists and four-wheeling fanatics who use it as a passage to the backcountry, leads to the oft-photographed and otherworldly beauty of Dead Horse Point State Park Overlook.

On this night, law enforcement agents worried that Arellano might use it as a backdoor escape to a fretwork of deserted four-wheeling roads that could then deliver him to I-70. "I'm on 313 right now, just turned onto it," reports a state trooper monitoring traffic near the dinosaur park. "We should think about maybe sticking someone at Floy [Floy Wash, Utah]. If he's gone to Blue Hill Road, he could get out at Floy."

"There's that issue," replies another officer. "And we gotta cover 128"—the scenic byway hugging the Colorado River as it bends east, then north, out of Moab.

That trooper then expresses the need to "start locking the area down. We gotta set up a perimeter. Gotta set it up broad and then squeeze in."

That vast dragnet would prove unnecessary—in finding Arellano's car, at least. Around 10 p.m. that night, a Utah Highway Patrol helicopter spotted that Grand Am abandoned on a plateau beyond Potash Road. Arellano had left his car on Shafer Trail, a dozen miles south of the parking lot where he'd shot me.

With a roughly fifteen-minute lead on the legions of police and deputies who would soon compose one of the largest manhunts in Utah state history, he steered away from Moab, away from the checkpoints, into the outback. He was familiar with Moab, having participated in past Easter Jeep Safaris. A forty-year-old with few friends, limited prospects, and no housing, having just been evicted by his mother, my best guess is that he was feeling aggrieved—picked on and singled out, like the protagonist in "Police on My Back," the song written in 1967 by Eddie Grant (of "Electric Avenue" fame) and then given new life in 1980 when it was covered by the Clash.

News accounts in the wake of the shooting mentioned his criminal history—mainly misdemeanors. There was an arrest for assault somewhere in there and a theft charge. But mostly it was minor stuff: traffic violations, some weed. Reading over his low-level priors, you would not peg Lance as someone who was particularly dangerous. Here's a partial list of his infractions and misdemeanors: *following too closely*, 1992; *no mud flaps*, Sandy City, 1999; *cutting corners*, Sandy City, 1999; *failure to yield the right of way at a stop sign*, South Salt Lake City, 2004; *failure to illuminate rear registration plate*, Mapleton City, 2008; *possession of marijuana and drug paraphernalia* (numerous times).

Reviewing those offenses, the fines they generated, and the endless succession of failures to appear, bench warrants, forfeited bail, you can almost feel the flame being turned up under his anger, his smoldering resentment. On many of those occasions, Arellano was driving on a suspended license, or lacked registration or proof of insurance, or all the above. So he'd get rung up on those charges too. Further compounding his problems, he often didn't bother showing up for court dates, leading to still more warrants for his arrest.

Here was a guy whose stepfather was a cop alleged to have hit and traumatized him starting when the boy was thirteen. Arellano was disinclined to trust the police, who then—in his mind, at least—kept giving him reasons to dislike and despise them.

I'm not excusing him. I'm just trying to understand him—trying to fathom why his trip wire was strung so *tight* that warm November night. It's possible that he'd had a bellyful of this life and reached the point where he was beyond caring, no effs left to give. Even though his mother had forbidden him from taking the four-wheeler, forcing him to venture forth in the sorry-ass Pontiac with body damage on the driver's side and the window that only stayed up with duct tape, he was down for one final backcountry adventure. He was ready to go out with a bang—and, if it came to that, to take a cop with him.

Cue Brody, the chill ranger, tapping on the window, leading with kindness: *Are you OK? Do you need help?* But Arellano isn't fooled by the Mr. Nice Guy approach. Perhaps he's seen it before and doesn't trust it. And sure enough, after the genial officer mentions a few possible campsites, down comes the jackboot on his neck: *Can I see some ID?*

Perhaps if I'd just let him skate—told him to move along without running his plates and checking on that oddly familiar handle (*Michael Oher—where have I heard *that name?*)—we would have parted on peaceful terms. But who's to say that he, with his backpack full of canned goods and ammo and unresolved anger for police, would not have turned his wrath on the next peace officer to cross his path? Maybe I took one for the team that night.

"I Want My Ashes Scattered in Moab"

From an interview with Sandee Arellano, ex-wife of Lance, in 2024:

SANDEE ARELLANO: I think he was an adrenaline junky. 'Cause he would just do crazy stuff. He liked going down to that Moab Jeep Safari in the spring, where you get to go register for the trails. He went down for that a couple times. One year one of his friends bailed on him, and me being me, I'm like, "Fine, I'll go." I had anxiety attacks the entire time on those [trails]. Of course the carburetor kept choking out on a *steep* hill, and I was like, "I'll get out and walk." It's strange, but when we were younger and we talked about death, we agreed that we both wanted to be cremated. And his wish was always "I want my ashes scattered in Moab."

CHAPTER 16

MANHUNT

Arellano didn't have much of a head start—maybe fifteen minutes—before I got on the radio and the dispatchers set the wheels of a manhunt in motion. We don't know where he was hit, but we do know he was bleeding. Whatever his plan, if he had a plan, he would have felt a sense of urgency as he sped through the canyon.

But the road follows the river, and the river was not in a hurry, bending and about-facing and doubling back on itself. After passing a dinosaur tracks and petroglyph attraction, the Colorado goosenecks to the north before changing its mind two miles later and proceeding south again. For an attempted murderer on the lam, those meanders would've required frantic braking and then accelerating and brought on, I'm guessing, what F. Scott Fitzgerald called "the hot whips of panic."

Five minutes later, Arellano would've hauled ass past the Intrepid Potash plant for which the road is named, zipping past railroad cars that carry supplies to the mine. And then Potash Road is no more, asphalt giving way to the washboarded red dirt of Shafer Trail, which veers west away from the Colorado, then bends back toward the river around ten miles south at Thelma and Louise Point, the cliff from which those fictional fugitives took flight in a turquoise '66 Thunderbird. Arellano never got that far. After bumping along for a couple miles on Shafer Trail, he ditched the Pontiac and set off on foot.

Three years earlier at a Moab trailer park, a man with a rifle and handgun walked briskly toward a Grand County sheriff's deputy, who repeatedly warned him to stop and drop his weapons. But James Lewis Gaylord kept walking (his wife later described him as "suicidal"), reached for his handgun, and was shot dead by the deputy.

To process the scene of this shooting by one of his own men, then Grand County Sheriff Jim Nyland asked for help from the Weber County Sheriff's Office, renowned in the state for its excellent crime scene investigation unit. Recalling the superb job done by Weber County on that occasion, Nyland requested they return to Moab for this latest officer-related shooting.

CSI supervisor Sandra Ladd (now Grogan) got the call after midnight. Her presence was requested at the Poison Spider Mesa trailhead, where the crime scene was being preserved. Grogan and fellow CSI officer Angie Petersen covered the 275 miles in less than five hours, pulling into the gravel trailhead parking lot at 7:20 a.m. They climbed the rock face rising above the north side of the lot to videotape the "pristine scene," as Grogan put it in her report. They marked numerous pieces of evidence, including a mix of aluminum and brass shell casings, thirty-nine total. Winter weather had moved in, and high winds made it necessary for them to use metal wire, then rocks, to hold evidence markers in place.

Photographed and collected earlier in the morning were the bloodstained clothes EMTs had sheared off me. The CSI officers would later painstakingly count the number of bullet holes in each article of clothing, along with the placement of each hole. My white T-shirt was in especially rough shape, with two holes in the back, another just above the right hip area—Arellano's probable final shot at me—and two in the left arm: one where the bullet went in, the other where a large fragment exited.

In case you're curious, that shirt was a temple garment of the kind worn by many Latter-day Saints. Such garments are akin to religious vestments in other faiths—a Jewish prayer shawl, for instance, or a Muslim hijab. They're sacred to us, reminding us of commitments we've made to the Lord in the temple. On a simpler level, they serve as ever-present reminders to lead a modest and decent life, like Christ.

In my experience, temple garments provide subtle prompts—not always heeded, but I try—to choose the right path; to be a good person; to hold my family above all else, beside Heavenly Father himself; to work hard; and to lead an honorable life.

As the late Latter-day Saint Bishop J. Richard Clarke emphasized four decades ago in his essay "The Value of Work," we are obligated to "give full, honest effort to our jobs as though we owned the enterprise. . . . To do less is to live our lives unfulfilled." I'd always done my best to honor that

NINE MIRACLES

commitment to my job—part of which, it turned out, was training to be ready for an ambush.

And so, in an indirect but undeniable way, and even though the bullets passed right through them, the garments played a role in saving my life. But magic had nothing to do with it. Twenty-three of the thirty-nine shell casings found on the ground were aluminum .40-caliber Smith & Wesson rounds, manufactured by Federal Premium Ammunition. Those had come from my gun and were found "arranged around the passenger side of the vehicle (south) and back/rear of the vehicle (west)," according to Grogan's report. The remaining sixteen bullets, of three different varieties, had been fired from "around the driver's side of the Ford F-150 and in front of the Ford."

That night, CSI officers Grogan and Petersen set up their ballistics laser to help visualize bullet paths, a technique that assists them in identifying the positions of shooters and victims. I wasn't talking at the time in my coma, so investigators were especially eager to hear the officers' findings. But the converters in their vehicles couldn't generate sufficient voltage to run the unit, Grogan recalls. So they used "trajectory dowels and a laser pointer" instead. The CSI officers were able to deduce that shots were fired from the passenger's side of the Ford F-150, "passing through the interior of the truck, and exiting out the driver's side, possibly hitting the north natural rock wall." While the truck's doors were closed when they arrived, Grogan noted, the laser information showed that "the front driver's door must have been open at some time during the exchange of shots being fired."

They also determined that I'd fired rounds from a position very low to the ground, "1 foot 10 inches to 6 inches." I have no recollection of this, but according to the report, I'd put at least one slug in the left rear tire and one in the bumper. (Cut me some slack—I was passing out!) "When setting up the laser," Grogan wrote, "it appears these shots were fired by an individual on the ground behind the rear of the vehicle." The shell casings found in that area were mine.

Again, I have no memory of firing rounds from that low vantage, but it's clear from Grogan's report (which I didn't read until May 2024) that I did. That's where I'd backpedaled—stumbled, really—before collapsing onto my backside. My best guess is I was sitting on the ground, on the verge of passing out, leaning back, legs splayed, firing between my feet.

Tony White was one of my guardian angels that night. You remember Lieutenant White, who doubled as both my supervisor and my firearm training instructor. He has some pretty strong hunches about what happened in that parking lot.

I spent a lot of time on the range with White. Mind you, we were required to qualify twice yearly on handgun and shotgun. Rifles weren't approved or issued until nearly ten years later. One of these qualifications was under daylight conditions, the other under low-light/night conditions coupled with some sort of stress shooting exercise or scenario. I can still hear him lecturing us to not let our "car become our casket." Once out of the vehicle, he emphasized, it could be used for cover and concealment. White also instructed, "Fire on your assailant what they present to you." And if that meant shooting someone's foot under a pickup because you couldn't see the rest of the body, "that's what you fire on to save your life."

"To this day," he told an interviewer in 2024, "I'm pretty confident Brody fired rounds at the lower legs and feet of his assailant." He based that conclusion on the findings of CSI officers Grogan and Petersen, who on their second day in Moab "processed" Arellano's car, which had "damage," they noted, "to the front driver's side area: front bumper, driver's side quarter panel, and driver's side mirror."

Investigators had already located small amounts of blood on the trunk of the Grand Am and on the inside back driver's side door handle. There was blood inside the car, but the CSI officers had to search for it. The floor mat under the steering wheel had been turned upside down, they noted. Beneath the mat were leaves with apparent blood on them, and they found more blood "on the front" of the floor mat. No blood was found on the driver's seat, the steering wheel, the seat belt, or the "gear shift knob." That's what persuaded White that I had injured Arellano in a lower leg or foot.

Grogan and Petersen were asked to attend a "team leader debrief" that evening on Saturday, November 20, 2010, at Moab Fire House. Fourteen years later, Grogan remembers that meeting vividly. Of the scores of people attending, including team leaders and commanders, they were the only two women in the room. No one was rude or hostile, but at that briefing, and during their three days in Moab in general, she picked up on an undercurrent of resentment. "Just kind of like this air of 'Why are they here?'" she recalls. "'What are they doing that I can't do?'"

When she was asked at the briefing where the suspect had been shot, all eyes turned to them. Sandra explained that the only place she'd found blood in the Grand Am was on the floorboard and nowhere else inside the car. Based on that, she told the assembled officers and deputies, and the trajectory of where I was shooting—"especially toward the end," she recounts, "when his shots were all very low"—it seemed most logical to her that Arellano was hit in the leg or legs.

And how was that reply received? "They didn't like that," Grogan recalls. "They were like, 'No, he's mortally wounded,' and I just said, 'OK, you can say that, but all I see is blood on the floorboard. . . . I'm not saying that Brody didn't mortally wound him, but I also can't say he did.'"

After collecting some of his belongings, it appears Arellano set out on foot, leaving a blood trail. "It went for quite some time," recalls Grogan. "But they were blood drops; it wasn't like arterial spurt, or projected blood, as we call it now." The fugitive immediately bushwhacked off the trail, moving onto terrain that was relatively smooth for a few hundred yards but quickly turned rugged and inhospitable.

Resuming their search the following morning, agents made another key discovery. During the night, Arellano had moved another two miles south, back toward the river, taking refuge in a hideaway among some boulders and within sight of a remote wilderness lodge called Caveman Ranch.

There, stashed in a crack between rocks, he'd left behind a Ruger .22 wood stock rifle, along with a frameless Coleman "Max" backpack whose contents included a bag of several dozen .22 shells. On the outside of the pack, tucked under two straps, was a fleece-lined zip-up jacket shell. Inside were five tins of tuna, five cans of soup, a box of Ritz crackers, and a jar of peanut butter. Wedged under a nearby rock was a wadded-up purple long-sleeved T-shirt that told its own story.

That shirt featured a small rhinoceros stitched over a logo that said, "Stolen Classics." It also had a hole near the left armpit, possibly where a bullet had passed through. The left sleeve of the shirt had been torn off and was saturated with blood. Police surmised Arellano had used the sleeve as a tourniquet. The area of the shirt covering the left armpit was also dark-stained, indicating that Arellano had been bleeding from a nearby wound before tearing the arm off his shirt.

Agents found more blood near the waist of the backpack. The suspect also left behind a black stretch beanie hat and a .40-caliber handgun holster with no handgun in it. Wherever he was, Arellano was still armed, still dangerous.

Why leave food, warm clothing, and a rifle behind? Grand County Sheriff Jim Nyland speculated that Arellano had stopped to minister to his wounds when he heard or saw law enforcement agents nearby. "I think that our teams were getting close," he told reporters. "I think that he panicked and just left the stuff to try to get away."

The discovery of those items led authorities to focus the search on a more specific area, a triangle whose easternmost side was formed by the river. Sharpshooters took up positions on ridges overlooking the triangle. SWAT teams were on standby. Bloodhounds ranged over the rocks with far more ease than their biped handlers. A trio of helicopters searched from above, one equipped with a thermographic camera able to pick up infrared radiation—the heat generated, for instance, by a fleeing suspect.

One of the chopper pilots combing the desert from above was a private citizen from St. George, Utah. The moment he learned that a ranger had been shot, Jeremy Johnson volunteered to search for the fugitive in his own helicopter. It was only after a day in the air that Johnson learned the name of the wounded officer. He'd befriended a fellow redhead named Brody Young when they served on an LDS mission in Missouri some fifteen years earlier.

"They told me it was Brody Young, and I asked how old he was," he informed the *Salt Lake Tribune*. "Then I saw his picture." At that point, Jeremy told the reporter, "It got really personal. I'm more pissed off now. I'm really motivated to find this guy.... Anyone that knows Brody knows he's a really happy, funny guy. He's really a kind person. Doesn't have a mean bone in his body."

Down below, in twin-hulled boats marked "State Park Ranger," my colleagues plied the Colorado River just in case

Arellano had concluded that wading into those fifty-degree waters offered his best chance of escape.

This was the weekend before Thanksgiving, but that didn't stop law enforcement agents from pouring into Moab to join the manhunt. A *Salt Lake Tribune* story mentioned the unsettling juxtaposition of armored SWAT vehicles taking up parking stalls at the City Market grocery store. "It's strange to have so much law enforcement in Moab," the manager of a nearby bookstore told the reporter. "It's usually so quiet and peaceful."

Over two hundred officers arrived from Utah, Arizona, and Colorado. Most of their names ended up on a whiteboard in Nyland's office. He never did wipe that board clean. It ended up at the fire department, where for twelve years, the board went unused because firefighters never could bring themselves to erase the names of those who came and assisted with the search. To do so would have been, in their eyes, disrespectful.

Finally, a few years ago, Moab fire chief T. J. Brewer gave me the board, which now hangs in my office. Every so often, I read over those names with profound appreciation. I remain grateful to every one of those officers and their families. It's not like they were pitching in to help someone move into a new apartment. They were putting themselves in harm's way. Again and again. This part of the world was custom made for concealment. Fissures in the sandstone erode, over millennia, into cracks wide enough to hide a man. The terrain they were searching was a jumbled

Mars-scape of boulders, draws and gullies, deep crevices, and hidden caves.

Nyland mentioned one officer who discovered a cave with a low entrance. To squeeze in, the man had to remove his pack and bulletproof vest, lay down his rifle, and crawl into that void with his flashlight, hoping there wasn't an armed fugitive awaiting him. Multiply that single effort by, say, five hundred. "It's going to be difficult," said the sheriff.

Officers didn't just clear every cave, crack, crevice, and crevasse they came across. They waded through miles of dense stands of tamarisk along the riverbank. They searched every freight car on the tracks between Highway 191 and the Intrepid Potash plant, along with the seven-thousand-foot-long Bootlegger railroad tunnel.

If Saturday morning's discovery of a rifle, backpack, and makeshift tourniquet gave searchers a shot of morale, that boost was wearing off by nightfall, when Nyland allowed at a news conference, "Today, we didn't get a whole lot accomplished. We ran out of daylight."

But Sunday morning brought news: despite overnight rains, searchers had discovered footprints leading west from Arellano's hideaway and impromptu field hospital. The tracks pointed toward a distinctive, looming landform, an elevated red rock formation jutting up above the river. Perhaps two hundred feet across, it stretches from Caveman Ranch nearly half a mile to the north, its spine studded with towers of fractured cliff rock, like scales on a dragon. The scales stop at the far end of the formation, where the rock grows smooth and bears an uncanny resemblance—from the air, at least—to a hammerhead shark. Inhospitable as it appeared, the Dragonback Hammerhead, as this landform shall henceforth be known, must have called out like a siren to Arellano, who knew that it offered countless places to hide . . . or to lie waiting in ambush.

However, Sunday's search was cut short by a storm that moved in late afternoon, bringing rain and gusting winds. "The weather moved in on us," said Nyland, sounding determined but weary. "We had one area we were really in particular interested in. We tried to move into that area and as soon as we moved in, it started raining, the wind started blowing. I know we didn't complete the assignment tonight we wanted to." That said, he expressed confidence that Arellano was still somewhere within the established search perimeter: "We feel there's not any possible way for him to leave the area without us knowing."

Also taking a lead role in the manhunt, along with Sheriff Nyland, was his San Juan County counterpart, Mike Lacy, who told the *Salt Lake Tribune*, "You could have 1,000 people, and you couldn't search the whole area." Twelve years earlier, Lacy had helped in the Four Corners manhunt after a trio of antigovernment extremists stole a water truck. Dale Claxton, a police officer in Cortez, Colorado, tried to pull them over. Before he could even exit his car, one of the men got out of the truck and shot him nineteen times with a high-powered rifle. The suspects fled into the Utah desert, where all were eventually found, dead by their own hand. "I walked within 15 feet of one of the men's bodies, twice, and didn't see him," Lacy told the *Tribune*. It's possible, he added, that Arellano "could have slipped into a crack. We could walk right by him and not know."

The following is an article from the *Deseret News*, November 23, 2010:

Tired searchers continue efforts to locate fugitive gunman near Moab

MOAB—After four days of thoroughly searching Moab's backcountry, investigators have decided to "change the direction of the search," for a man charged with aggravated attempted murder.

Lance Arellano was charged Tuesday in 7th District Court with trying to kill state parks and recreation ranger Brody Young, 34, according to the Grand County Sheriff's office. Young received at least three gunshot wounds and remains in serious condition at a Colorado hospital. A warrant has been issued for Arellano's arrest.

Grand County Sheriff Jim Nyland said at a press conference Tuesday evening that SWAT teams will be on call, and deputies will be set up around the perimeter, but the foot patrols that have marked the past four days of the manhunt will be discontinued.

"Until we get another lead, there's no reason to have that many people in that area."

Nyland said it's possible Arellano may still be in the backcountry. He also said it's possible Arellano may have slipped through the perimeter or may have died.

And the following appeared the next day in the *Salt Lake Tribune* headline:

Sheriff on Moab shooter: "If he's still alive, he will be found"

MOAB—The helicopters that took over the skies earlier this week were gone Wednesday. So, too, were the hounds that had been tracking through the desert.

After five days of searching for Lance Leeroy Arellano, the man suspected of shooting state park ranger Brody Young outside of Moab last week, officials have significantly scaled back the manhunt.

During another night of freezing temperatures, snow coated the red rock valley Wednesday morning.

Police believe Young's shooter is either dead or will be caught.

"If he's still alive, he will be found," said San Juan Sheriff Mike Lacy, whose agency has been assisting in the search.

About 30 officers will keep watch over the rugged area where Arellano was believed to have been, said Grand County Sheriff Jim Nyland. A scaled-back search effort will continue in the desert "until we're satisfied that he may no longer be down there," the sheriff said.

Then the December 2, 2010, issue of the *Moab Times-Independent* said the following:

SEARCH FOR SUSPECTED SHOOTER TURNS UP NO NEW LEADS

The helicopters and SWAT teams may have left Moab last week, but Grand County Sheriff Jim Nyland says the search for the man police believe shot Utah State Parks Ranger Brody Young is continuing.

Searchers found footprints, a backpack and a .22-caliber rifle in an area known as Caveman Ranch, about 22 miles southwest of Moab, but over the next three days, no further evidence of Arellano was found, and the search was scaled back on Nov. 22.

Said Nyland, "He just kind of disappeared off the face of the earth."

Chapter 17

ALONG CAME THE SWIRLY

Let us take a moment, before proceeding with our narrative, to once again give it up for Wendy, who, in addition to her daily debriefs of a platoon of doctors and nurses, simultaneously succeeded in the more important task of building a figurative fortress around our children, keeping them comforted and on an even keel during an incredibly scary and uncertain time.

And there were her emails, that series of upbeat dispatches that went out to family members at frequent, if irregular, intervals. "If I have to choose between emailing or going for a run," she explained in one of them, "the email always loses." And yet she was prolific in those dispatches from the ICU. In addition to leaning on that upbeat oeuvre to tell this story—especially the parts where I was in a coma—I've found myself rereading those emails and smiling and falling harder still for this woman, who would sit at a laptop late at night in a strange condo, the weight of the world on her shoulders, an advocate for everyone but herself, tapping out these breezy, sometimes stream-of-consciousness accounts that reassured our loved ones, lightening their burden even if it meant adding to hers.

NINE MIRACLES

Wendy is both a voracious reader and a strong writer, as evidenced by, among other things, her skill at using understatement to darkly comic effect: "This past weekend was a bit more exciting than planned"—and, farther down in the same email—"He decided to push his heart rate up a notch" (to a life-threatening 180 beats per minute).

While taking a recent stroll through those emails, I had newfound respect for Wendy's ability to capture the often-paradoxical nature of life—"Man, does time fly & drag"—and her knack for translating often impenetrable medical terminology into language accessible to the layperson: "There appeared to be a bunch of fluid hanging out in places it shouldn't. . . . Brody has an infection in one of the muscles in his groin & a pocket of no-good goop in his gut."

In addition to that inspired alliteration, she could always be counted on to provide perspective, a level set: "Please remember that this is a positive experience. Brod is doing well. He is a miracle! He is getting better slowly but surely. Please do not be worried or sad. We are being watched over by the best caretaker there is!"

She didn't just mark milestones: "Thursday he made it all day without any help from the ventilator. . . . Brod got to eat real food this weekend. They removed the feeding tube from his nose & he is now in charge of getting his manly figure back." She did it with flair and panache and some superb similes, such as this description of what happened to my body when the edema finally subsided: "He went from looking like the Stay Puft Marshmallow Man to one of the California Raisins."

But her knack for comparisons reached its acme, its apotheosis, a few days after Christmas, when she likened the most recent disruption in our lives to being turned upside down and having our heads dunked in a cosmic Kohler commode: "Just when we thought we had a tiny bit of control—felt like we were the least bit prepared, along came the swirly."

She was referring to the shocking news we got on the eve of Christmas Eve.

Wendy had an excellent plan for December 23. She was going to load the crew in the car, bring me an early dinner, bolt over to Moab so the kids could get a taste of home—see friends, sleep in their own beds, unwrap a couple early Christmas presents—then head back to Grand Junction in time to spend Christmas Eve with Dad. Before leaving the condo, she called me at the hospital, asking me what I wanted to eat. I was hopped up on opioids and told her what the nurse had just told me: "Hey, they said I could leave!" That's right, I continued. I was being discharged from the hospital the next day.

When she heard those words, Wendy's first thought was "Wow, what drug is he on now?" Because the news made no sense. She'd been told a week earlier by my main doctor that if things continued to go smoothly, I might get to go home *at the end of January*. We weren't quite to the end of December.

Yeah, I'd been doing well with my physical therapy. Still, it seemed wildly premature for them to be booting me from the hospital a week and a half after I'd emerged from my medically induced coma and a day after doctors had performed a decannulation—pulling out the trach tube and sewing up the little hole in my neck for good.

Wendy had me pass the phone to the nurse, who confirmed the news. She needed to pick me up by 10:30 the next morning. That meant she needed to clear out all her and the kids' possessions from the loaner condo at the retirement village. They'd been accumulating stuff for six weeks—including a bike trailer and the Bob, the indestructible baby jogger she'd pushed over almost every square foot of Grand Junction.

To get everything, she would need a U-Haul trailer. "In that case," said our friends Dr. Robert Kloepper and his wife, Jill Buchanan, who happened to be at the hospital with me, "why don't you use the empty U-Haul trailer hitched to our car in the hospital parking lot right now?"

"Wait, what?" asked Wendy.

The Kloeppers were moving to Oregon. They were in Grand Junction to pick up a U-Haul and pull it back to Moab. At 8:30 p.m., they backed the trailer up to the cottage and helped Wendy load it. One of the last items on board was the Christmas tree. Then they drove that load back to Moab. "It was like I was drowning," Wendy remembers, "and they showed up in a boat."

Kloepper is an orthopedic surgeon. He seemed as confused as we were by the hospital's decision to discharge me. We never did figure out who made that call or what the rush was to get me out of there. Maybe the discharge office was feeling the heat from the insurance company. Maybe, because it was a holiday weekend, the hospital administrators on duty that day were . . . not members of the varsity team. Or maybe someone had seen the 1998 Disney movie *I'll Be Home for Christmas* and thought they were doing us a favor.

Which, on one level, they were. I'd been shot exactly five weeks earlier. As the darkness closed in that night, and the cement settled more heavily, and my spirit hovered in equipoise between two worlds, I was yanked back to *this* one, back to life, by the thought of four people. And now we'd be spending Christmas together at home! It was a wonderful blessing.

It was also a terrible idea and a big mistake. I had no business going home, as I overheard Wendy sharing with someone high up at the hospital: "He's been conscious for five days. He got out of intensive care three days ago. What the hell are you thinking?" She called various departments at St. Mary's but couldn't reach anyone with enough juice to overturn the decision. It was the day before Christmas. A lot of people were already on holiday. We are churchgoing folk, members of a faith that puts a premium on peace, but Wendy was ready to fight someone that morning, and I don't mean argue with them.

And that was *before* I was discharged. Afterward, we beelined for the nearest Walgreens, where we were told that it would not be possible to fill prescriptions for painkillers because of some problems with paperwork. Would it be possible for us to try again on Monday? When I say "us" in this case, I mean Wendy, who fought that war of attrition while I sat like a crash test dummy in the passenger seat. But the drugs I was on were wearing off, and that was a problem.

After a half hour, Wendy called in a one-woman cavalry named Bernadette Christiansen, a nurse case manager specializing in workers' compensation cases. That she'd been assigned to me was another stroke of excellent fortune. Bernadette has the kindest eyes and a warm smile, but if you are an obstacle between one of her clients and their proper care, she will come at you like a wolverine. She drove into her office, then called Walgreens, armed with my file, and straightened things out. "OK, we're good to go," said the pharmacy staff. "The prescriptions should be ready in forty-five minutes." Which was good, because the pain was flaring up in my left arm . . . and gut, and butt, and groin, and also along the zipper scar from my neck to my navel—the scar that would become infected shortly after we got home and pop open at the top like that scene in *Alien*.

But that was still two weeks away. One hour and forty-five minutes after Walgreens said the prescriptions would be ready, Wendy called Bernadette to inform her that the store was now saying that three of the seven of them were not authorized. Alas, the workers' compensation staffers who could green light that authorization were gone for the weekend. Would it be possible for us to return on Monday?

Bernadette promptly left messages for the insurance adjuster, an RN, and the Workers' Compensation Fund case management coordinator. She called Walgreens, then got in her car and drove there to underscore the urgency of this matter. She had Walgreens staff provide her with the number for Express Scripts, a pharmacy benefit manager, emphasizing to the person who answered the phone that she, Bernadette, had spoken with the adjuster, who had assured her all the prescriptions were authorized. After consulting their file, the Express Scripts staffer informed her that—hey, what do you know?—the three prescriptions in question *were* authorized. "Please tell that to Walgreens," said Bernadette. They did, and I got my pills. It was as simple as that. That was three hours of our lives we'll never get back. It was also a single example of countless battles Wendy and Bernadette fought for me.

I slammed some painkillers, and we put Grand Junction in the rearview mirror. I'm sure I felt happiness as we crossed the border back into Utah, getting closer to home. What I also felt, and recall vividly, was the feeling of dizziness, vertigo, and nausea. Wendy was only doing the speed limit—seventy-five miles per hour—along that stretch of I-70. But I'd been in a hospital bed for six weeks; to me it felt like we were hitting hyperdrive on the Millennium Falcon. I'd been so still for so long, and now everything was moving so fast.

Signal fires had been lit, text messages sent. Word arrived in Moab a few hours before our arrival that the Youngs were

NINE MIRACLES

headed home. Among those to hear the news was Linda Hugentobler, another of the Wendy's Walkers, who converged on our house with her husband and children and several other families. Working with their fellow ministering angels, the Kloeppers, they unloaded the U-Haul, then tidied and got the place ready for us. One thoughtful soul donated a power recliner—a La-Z-Boy on steroids—which awaited me in the living room. I wasn't yet ready to take the stairs to our bedroom, so that plush recliner also served as my bed for the next few weeks.

It was a mellow Christmas at the Young household. Wendy loaded up the Bob and got a run around the neighborhood while I sawed logs in the La-Z-Boy. I'm not sure if it was Christmas or the next day that someone knocked on the door while Wendy and the kids were out. After fumbling to find the correct button that would move the recliner to "upright," then marshaling my puny core strength to stand and reaching for my trusty cane, I tottered and hobbled to the door, where I was greeted by the sight of my beloved aunt and uncle: Robert Neslen (remember the ostrich-skin-booted landlord Wendy and I worked for?) and his wife, Tammy. Technically, they're *Wendy's* aunt and uncle and I just borrow them, but the distinction faded a long time ago.

They hadn't seen me since the shooting. They told me afterward they had no idea what to expect. They thought Wendy would answer the door and that I might be in a bed, semiconscious, still hooked up to some tubes. But the door opened, and it was me standing there, and in that first moment, I could register their shock at my appearance. For a month I'd been taking nourishment through a tube in my nose. Normally I'm around 230 pounds. At that point, I was down probably fifty pounds. And then, as Tammy recalls, "Bob just started bawling."

I was standing there alive, which left him incredulous and grateful in equal measure. As we hugged, I whispered, "Don't squeeze me." I tottered back to my chair, and we sat and visited, and Bob cried some more. "You shouldn't be here," he told me before asking, "Why do you think you're still here?" He meant here among the living rather than here at our humble casa on Park Drive in Moab. "I don't know, but I intend to find out," I said. That, at least, is the reply Tammy remembers me giving.

Eventually, I would turn my attention to trying to tackle those looming existential riddles such as *How did I survive? Why was I spared? What is my purpose now?* In that moment, however, I faced more immediate, small-bore questions, such as *Who will help me get to the bathroom, which is up a half-flight of stairs in our split-level home? Who will prepare my meals and bring them to me? Who will keep track of my seven prescriptions and bring my pills at the correct time?* Until I crushed some more physical therapy and gained some more function, the answer was clear—Wendy.

Wendy had begun this year in the throes of a very difficult pregnancy requiring dozens of ultrasounds in her final trimester. The birth of our youngest, Jag, was a radiant, beaming bright spot in what had been a "terrible, horrible, no good, very bad" stretch, to borrow from the children's book by author Judith Viorst and illustrator Ray Cruz.

Yes, I was out of the hospital. But Wendy's life was about to get markedly harder, not easier. In addition to taking care of her three children under the age of six, she would be her husband's caretaker. I'd become her fourth child.

"I think Wendy had more stress once you came home," Jennifer Taylor later shared with me. "I remember talking to her, and she was like, 'I can't do all this.' She was so overwhelmed. That's when her stress really spiked. Sending you home for Christmas would have been a happy ending if this was Hollywood. But in actual real life, it was hideous."

The following is an excerpt of a Wendygram sent December 28, 2010:

> So yes, we are home. No, there are not any aliens dressed like us floating around the town—for those of you who are wondering.
>
> We enjoyed a very mellow Christmas—I even got to go running with the kids while Brod napped!
>
> Brod continues to improve each day. He enjoys physical therapy and wound care treatment from Home Health (professional in-home care) & short walks around the block. He still has a long road ahead, but he has made it pretty darn far at this point! We will still be traveling to [Grand] Junction probably weekly, but Stry gets to go back to school. (I am not sure who is more excited about that!)

We just wanted all of you to know how grateful we are to each of you for your love and support. I have learned that even though I think I can handle everything on my own—I can't. (Please don't tell anyone though.)

THANK YOU THANK YOU THANK YOU!

We hope that you truly enjoy this holiday season. We are so grateful to a loving God that truly watches out for his children—even if it is not always in the way that we would choose.

Merry Christmas & Happy New Year

Love, Brod, Wen, & the gang

Chapter 18

STRONG AT THE BROKEN PLACES

◉

Sure, it was a shock to get the boot from St. Mary's. But it's not like they sent me home empty-handed. Like a losing contestant on *The Price Is Right*, I left with a pair of swell parting gifts. Not Rice-A-Roni or a year's supply of Turtle Wax but rather (to be read aloud in the voice of longtime game show announcer Johnny Olson), "How about this handsome, water-resistant SHOWER BENCH, with a load-bearing weight up to 250 pounds! And when you've struggled to your feet, après shower, get around the house with the help of this ADJUSTABLE ALUMINUM CANE—with a nonskid rubber tip!"

The cane, while helpful, was also a symbol and reminder of my invalid status, my decrepitude. I couldn't wait to stop needing it. But it proved essential for me in those unsteady first few weeks. "Brody really was like a ninety-five-year-old man," recalls Wendy, who can still picture me hobbling about. I slept in the La-Z-Boy on the main floor—which did nothing for the bedsore / bald spot on the back of my head—and lived for the day I could make it up the eight steps to the bathroom without requiring help from another adult. I was a stooped, shuffling shell of my former self. No wonder my kids felt the need to arm themselves.

There's a lot of Scandinavian blood on Wendy's side of the family and a dash on mine as well. As we've told the kids, mostly in jest, "We're Vikings!" That's how they ended up with a modest armory of plastic battle-axes and swords.

After we all came back to the Moab house, Stryder and Jayde made it part of their nightly ritual to bring those weapons to bed with them—along with their Star Wars light sabers. They weren't playing, though. It wasn't a game to them. They slept with those "weapons" to protect us if someone came into our house. They weren't worried that I was going to die of my wounds by this point; they were afraid that the bad man was going to come back and try to finish me off. Their nightly call to arms "was the sweetest thing but also the most heartbreaking thing," Wendy remembers. For our kids to feel unsafe in their own home—"that was rough."

Preattack, I'd seen myself as protector and provider for my crew. Those were my primary roles. Now that I couldn't perform them, I realized how central they'd been to my identity. I realized how much I wanted them back. I was determined once again to be that person, that husband, that dad. But this comeback wasn't going to happen in a hurry. It was going to be long, painstaking, fraught with setbacks. Meanwhile, it was a struggle for me to walk around the block.

A couple weeks after I got home, Wendy drove me back to Grand Junction for my first appointment with Dr. Robert McLaughlin, the occupational medicine physician. Working together, we would outline a long-term treatment plan, with the goal of my regaining as much function as possible, then returning to my job.

McLaughlin had created a niche in his area of practice as the doctor who saw "extra bad cases," as he put it. So that's how I ended up in his office. On several occasions, McLaughlin mentioned that I had the option of going on full-time disability and never working again. But I had zero interest in that alternative. (I say that with compassion and respect for those whose injuries leave them no choice but to go on disability. Unlike them, I had a choice.) I genuinely loved my work—interacting with and helping members of the public in our state's peerless public lands. It had always felt like a privilege, more than a job, to spend my working hours in the backcountry or on the Colorado. I couldn't wait to get back in the field, back on the water.

Four years after our first meeting, McLaughlin was asked by an interviewer what he recalled of it. His memorable reply: "I couldn't believe he wasn't dead." He'd treated plenty of patients with gunshot wounds, he added, but none with nearly as many. He mentioned the bullet in my left lung and the ones that "went through [my] belly and caused injuries to [my] stomach, small colon and large bowel." He reflected on how fortunate it was that the slug in my left arm hadn't found the nearby brachial artery, which would've caused me to bleed out right there in the parking lot.

Rob was incredulous that the slug in the L2 region of my spine hadn't somehow done more damage—"You look at it and go, 'How did it get in there? How did he not get paralyzed?'" And he was even more incredulous that the slug that came to rest beside my heart did so little harm: "To look at it, I mean, you just can't believe it. Where the bullet is sitting. The left ventricle is the [chamber] that pumps blood to the body. So it's thicker, bigger, stronger. That's where the bullet is. [Dr. Sara Pereira] just had a little repair there. . . . If he got shot in any other area of the heart, it probably just blows it to nothing, and he dies within minutes. . . . You hear this guy's story, but you don't believe it. That's what it comes down to. There's no way."

McLaughlin was also struck by the way I'd "prepared" myself for the attack, with firearms training and fitness. "He's a survivor," McLaughlin told that interviewer in 2015. "It's a mental outlook, and Brody just decided he wasn't going anywhere. He wasn't giving up. This was not going to stop him."

During our first appointment, he told me it would take a good year for me to get back on my feet. "You're wrong," I told him. "It won't take half that long." He wasn't wrong. "The journey of a thousand miles begins with a single step," proclaimed Chinese philosopher Lao Tzu. Looking back on my return to near-full health as its own thousand-mile trek—and sticking to that Taoist metaphor—I'd guesstimate that I took nine hundred miles' worth of steps at the Mountain Land Physical Therapy clinic, about a quarter mile south of our house in Moab.

It was always nice to see the warm, welcoming faces of clinic director Jim Lewis and his fellow therapists—even though they traffic in torture and even though just setting foot on the premises ensured an hour or so of anaerobic anguish. In other words, they're excellent at their jobs, which is to get us to work through discomfort and to discover new limits on each visit. It was difficult work, sometimes excruciating. But I welcomed the challenge: the harder I worked in PT, the easier life would be later.

Exertion and movement would make me whole again. Wendy understood this better than I did at first. That's why sometimes when I'd ask for a glass of water, she would instruct me to stand up and get it myself. If she felt I'd been too immobile, spot-welded to the La-Z-Boy for too long, she might direct me to get off my atrophied ass and play with the children for ten minutes. At the time, it struck me as a trifle mean. But she was right. Bringing me water when I could get it myself was not only "perpetuating her own enslavement," as a friend put it; it was slowing my recovery.

Even after I graduated to spending nights back in my own bed, my world was pretty small. I'd go to physical therapy, then come home. Go to a doctor's appointment, then come home. I was at home a lot, and certain people noticed: "I *like* Brody's 'new job,'" proclaimed three-year-old Jayde when I returned from physical therapy late one morning in time for lunch with her.

The first few months after I returned home from the hospital were an absolute grind for Wendy, whose sacrifices I will dwell on more deeply in a later chapter. She fed and dressed and washed me, drove me to appointments, and helped me get to the bathroom—all the while performing similar services for three young children.

But our temporary new routine also brought its own rewards, its blessings. During my time in ICU, it had been very difficult for my kids to not be in a room with me or talk to me for weeks on end. Now that I was out—of the coma and the hospital—we were making up for lost time. The children and I and Wendy frequently had these regular snuggle sessions just before bedtime, which doubled as "Open Mic Night." They were free to ask me about what had happened, and I answered as honestly as I could. Stryder and Jayde asked about the different places I'd been shot, how much it hurt, if I was scared, and if I had cried. ("A lot," "yes," and "sometimes" were my replies to the last three.)

This was at a time when the search for Arellano, while scaled down, was still ongoing. Jayde and Stryder were understandably and intensely interested in his whereabouts and his intentions toward us. If he was still alive, I told them, he probably had no interest in us. Lance wasn't mad at me, I elaborated, so much as he had an intense dislike for perhaps *any* law enforcement officer who stopped to talk to him. Even though there's something deeply personal about shooting another person, let's face it, I never thought it was personal between him and me. I shared that last part with the kids. Other than him muttering "You got me" at one point, we never again spoke to each other once the shooting started.

I told them we'd learned that part of the reason he was upset was because a grown-up had mistreated him when he was a boy. I reminded them that no matter how he felt about me, I had forgiven him. We talked about how good it felt to forgive someone and how important it was to be brave and to keep trying when it was our turn to do something hard, even if things weren't going very well in the beginning. Mostly I worked to share my deep conviction that, regardless of what had happened to me, the world was still a good place—an amazing place! We had many conversations about that.

And then one morning in March, a year and four months after I was shot and a couple weeks after getting the green light from McLaughlin, I put on my ranger uniform and strode into the kitchen, where Stryder and Jayde were devouring cereal.

Stryder broke the silence: "What are you doing?"

I told them, "I'm going to work today. Gonna go work in the office."

Jayde: "What?"

"I'm going to go work in the office for a couple hours."

One Mississippi passed. Two Mississippis. Then they nodded and went back to wolfing down cereal. They were OK with me returning to work. That was a good moment.

My recovery was chronicled by nurse case manager extraordinaire Bernadette Christiansen, whose crisp updates every couple of weeks provide a distilled yet detailed account of my journey back to myself. The funny thing is, in the eighteen months I worked closely with her, she never once addressed me as "Mr. Young," but that's how I show up in her dispatches, like the subject of a *New York Times* story. Here I am in her initial report on the last day of 2010:

> Mr. Young reported that four bullets remain in his body. One is in the bottom of his left lung, one is close to his spine in the thoracic area behind his heart, one is near the L2 vertebra, and one is in the area of his right pelvis iliac crest.
>
> I asked Mr. Young what wounds the nurse from Community Nursing Services was currently treating. He reported he has a 1) bedsore on the back of his head that is doing well (about the size of a quarter), 2) a wound on the R upper forearm that is big but not deep, 3) and 4) two wounds on his belly, the bottom one is a concern (drains more) and one above the belly button, 5) 1 in the groin (small, a little drainage), and 6) R thigh (about three inches long, skinny then widens and gets skinny again), and 7) another one on the right buttock that is deep that is more of a concern.

I remember that bullet hole. It was a pain in the ass. She continues,

> On 1-10-11, Mr. Young saw Dr. Horiagan, Pulmonologist. Dr. H had a chest X-ray performed and discussed where the bullet remains in the left lung. He reported that the bronchoscope in the hospital showed it was not in an

airway. If that were to change, one of the first symptoms would be he would cough blood . . .

On 2/18/11 Mr. Young reported that Dr. Deering was very pleased with the healing in the left arm. Dr. Deering plans to take the rod out in June 2011, since arm is healing so well.

Or as my wife put it in a subsequent Wendygram,

His left arm is doing remarkably well. The bone shards have rallied around the rod and are starting to form a bone callus. Brod's surgeon said she has only seen this type of healing one other time. It may save him from having surgery again. It is still too early to determine. He has bits of shrapnel making their way to the surface of his arm as well.

Bernadette kept updates brief by dispensing with transitions and sometimes buried the lede, as on February 18, 2011: "He reported that there was a discussion about his being promoted and moving to Salt Lake City, but he and his family did not want to live in Salt Lake City. He explained that he is now able to achieve an erection."

I wasn't necessarily sharing with Bernadette or my doctors the extent to which I sometimes . . . overdid it, such as this misadventure detailed in a mid-March Wendygram:

> We nearly did him in on a bike-ride last week. (Mind you it was his first ride since the incident.) He was determined to ride with us to the music park down here. There are a few hills on the way. He did make it, but it took 4 days to recover! We are looking for an easier bike to ride. Unfortunately my train is already full. Jayde rides the tagalong followed by Jag in the chariot. I am afraid I will have to apply for a special permit if it gets any longer!

Indeed, the rig Wendy rolled in, with our little ones in tow, seemed to have sprung from the imagination of Dr. Seuss.

Despite regular, rigorous PT, my right quadriceps remained stubbornly atrophied and puny. My neurologist, Mitch Burnbaum, MD—who may or may not compose his memos while wearing a top hat—had thoughts: "It appears that this gentleman has a high femoral nerve injury, very possibly as the femoral nerve goes through iliopsoas. He also probably has a lateral femoral cutaneous nerve injury. He is reinnervating his muscles and that process can continue for 18–24 months. There is little he can do other than muscle-strengthening exercises. His loss of sensation may never return." Dr. Burnbaum was correct. I never did recover that quad—the ledge of muscle hanging over the knee. It's a grievous loss, but I can live with it.

Bernadette didn't limit herself to accounts of just my physical health, as we see in this mid-May entry:

> On 5-17-11, Dr. McLaughlin examined Mr. Young . . . and discussed how he was doing with issues related

to the person who shot him not yet being found. . . . Dr. McLaughlin recommended that Mr. Young go to the gun range and fire his gun. He indicated this would help with desensitization, and he would be able to evaluate how he felt being around the gun and the sound of shooting.

By that time, I was intensely curious to know how it would feel to strap on my duty belt and holster and fire at a target. At McLaughlin's recommendation, I headed out to the range with Tony White and Chief Quick. To my surprise and relief, it felt easy and natural and not scary. I wasn't conflicted or traumatized in the slightest. I never want to shoot another person again. But it was good to fire a round, feel the recoil, and know that I could still do the job. That was reassuring.

6-13-11: Mr. Young reported that he had worked 16 hours the past 2 weeks, 4 hours a day, four days a week, and he was able to come home and continue to do activities. He reported that he was still bike riding and hiking with the family. He reported that he had stopped taking Oxy-Contin the prior Tuesday, 6-7-11.

Weaning off the strong narcotic oxycodone hydrochloride (OxyContin) was harder than I thought it would be. That drug was an invaluable tool, masking massive amounts of pain after I was shot. It gave me relief and let me rest, let me heal. But I noticed, over time, that it also exacted a toll—and I'm not just referring to the dour handmaiden Madame

Constipation (for which I had a ready antidote. Thanks, MiraLAX!).

After a while, it felt like OxyContin was suppressing my personality, turning me into a zombie. Part of that is the way it reorients you. The drug wants very much to become the center of your universe. I was taking two a day, and I'd start jonesing for that second pill a good four, five, six hours before I was scheduled to pop it. Sometimes that long wait left me with a generalized full-body ache. I'd feel nauseous and break out in a cold sweat. Sometimes my hands shook while I waited. I had become dependent on the drug. It was tough to break that dependency, to banish the zombie. But I got there and felt a quickening after that—an acceleration in the journey back to myself.

Once in a while, however, that acceleration got a little out of control:

> Mr. Young reported he was on a raft on 6-13-11 in the late afternoon and the boat hit a large [hydraulic vortex] and wave. He reported he was holding on, flew up in the air, then came down pushing his bent arms backwards. He reported he heard a pop in the left shoulder. The upper half of his left upper arm became quite swollen.

Oops, tore my rotator cuff. On the bright side, during subsequent shoulder surgery, the doctor cleared out scar tissue that had been restricting my range of motion. Here's Wendy's highly technical summary:

> The surgery went well. It lasted about 3 hours. The doctors cut away lots of scar tissue & scoped out the shoulder. They were very pleased with how well the bone has healed in Brody's arm. They opted to not remove the rod . . . the reasoning for this is they did not want to take away Brody's bionic abilities! Just kidding—part of his rotator cuff healed over the area where they would have removed the rod. They would have had to cut the cuff to get the rod out. Which would have caused more problems.

A year after being shot, I was on the North Shore of Oahu enjoying a Thanksgiving vacation with extended family. We had a blast. But I may have overdone it yet again.

In a December 1, 2011, Wendygram, Wendy wrote,

> Does it ever just blow you away when you look at everything that has happened in the last year? Who would have thought that Brody's being shot would turn out to be such an incredible, positive experience?

Without context, the premise of that last question seems highly unlikely, deeply implausible. Under what circumstances, after all, could the damage done to me by Arellano be considered a positive thing?

As Hemingway put it, "The world breaks everyone and afterward many are strong at the broken places." The trials that tested but failed to destroy me and my loved ones made us stronger. They also created a thousand shining moments—opportunities for others to exhibit their compassion and charity and grace. In that sense, yes, the attack became "a tremendous blessing," as Wendy wrote: "We have been stretched and pushed and shoved until we thought we would burst and then something tremendous would happen and everything would be all right again. I think all of us, including Jag (22 months), have learned and grown a ton. There is an appreciation and strength between us now."

She tapped out that email from Hawaii. A year to the day after major surgery on my left arm, I used that wing to pull myself into countless waves in an epic bodyboarding session that left everyone thrashed but happy:

> Brod was right in the thick of it with all of us. He had a major advantage over the rest of us the next day as he was the only one with pain killers!
>
> At this time last year, Brody had undergone 3 big surgeries. They had opened him up from his collarbones to his navel, put the rod in his arm & rewired the electrical current of his heart.
>
> As of yesterday, he was released to return to work full-time—for a trial period. Who would have thought it even possible?
>
> Somewhere in my dreamy mind, I imagined everything would be back to normal by this time . . . I guess it's a new kind of normal. There's a lot we don't know, and we have no idea what will happen next.

Chapter 19

SKELETON MAGNET

In the spring of 2014, police in Provo announced an unsettling discovery. In the space of fifteen minutes, a hiker high up on 7,865-foot Kyhv Peak, then known as Squaw Peak, had discovered two unrelated sets of human remains. One of the deceased had leaped from a thousand-foot cliff. The other, six years later, had overdosed on pills, then sat down under a tree and died.

While those two departed were soon identified, the name of the hiker who found them never made it into the newspapers. That wasn't a problem for twenty-two-year-old Caleb Shumway, a Moab native and Eagle Scout who wasn't looking for any publicity. He was just trying to release some stress and get his heart rate up.

He'd arrived at the trailhead at 10:15 that morning, according to his report to the police, but quickly "broke off" the main trail and "started finding [his] own route"—blazing his own steeper, more technical path to the summit. From the time he exited the trail, Shumway couldn't explain the path he chose. "I was just kind of grabbing shrubs and pulling myself through," he recalled in 2024. He was in flow, his navigation unconscious: "It was decisions without a 'why' behind 'em. It was just 'Go here,' 'Go up this.'"

Not long after passing a pair of sealed-off caves, he traversed an ominous-looking outcropping of rock, then began the arduous climb up a steep drainage—the pathway worn by water flowing down the mountain. That's when he saw the first bone fragment, about the size of a shoehorn.

He didn't think much of it. "You're in the mountains," says Shumway. "You see bones." Then he saw another bone. This one he picked up. It didn't seem like it belonged to an animal, he recalls. Nor did the next several, as he proceeded up that drainage. Shumway soon came upon a pile of bones mixed among the slip rock and oak brush. He noticed human ribs, a hip bone, two femurs, a pair of shorts. Spying an odd-looking bowl filled with dried leaves, he says, "I picked it up and dumped the leaves out. It was actually the top of the skull. The rest of the skull had busted apart from it."

Time to call in some law. Hunting for cell reception, he climbed to the face of a cliff, got a couple bars, and phoned Provo police, describing what he'd found. They told him that they were sending officers up in a helicopter and that he should move to an open area where they could spot him. Moments after the call ended, he turned away from the cliff and saw a skeleton, propped casually against a tree, looking like it might come to life at any moment and strike up conversation, "like in the movie *Pirates of the Caribbean*," Shumway recalls. Those bones scattered in the drainage belonged to the cliff jumper. But on a ledge close to the intact skeleton,

Shumway discovered a bag in which police later found pills the man had used, they surmised, to take his own life.

I'm alive today because I was open to certain premonitions, intuitions, presentiments—various words that mean roughly the same thing but none perfectly capturing the pull, the inexplicable imperative I was feeling to take my firearms training *really* seriously. To embark on a cardio journey, to see how physically fit I could get. To leave the driver's side door of my truck open each time I made a contact in the backcountry, even though that wasn't in any training session or manual and my colleagues regarded it as kind of a quirk. I did things, took actions, without knowing precisely why.

What I discovered after the fact is that Shumway rolls that way too. He has a gift for tuning out the extraneous noise of the world, finding what Joseph Campbell called "the still place," where he did his best thinking and heard what was truly important. As a student at Utah Valley University in nearby Orem, Shumway made the drive over Rock Canyon, the trail leading to Kyhv Peak, as often as he could. Ever since he attended Provo's Missionary Training Center in 2011, before embarking on his two-year mission to New Zealand, he'd felt an almost magnetic pull toward that mountain. "There would be times I'd look at it" from the training center, he recalls, "and my mind would carry me off into the canyon."

Yes, getting to the summit was a terrific workout and an excellent adventure—especially since he often eschewed established trails, blazing his own, more challenging routes.

But after finding those human remains, solving for two families the mystery of what became of their loved ones, he suspected that he'd been drawn to that peak for a higher purpose. "Some people call it spiritual; some people call it weird," he says. "But I would say there is some sort of connection that our spirits have to the world around us."

Even before I ended up all over the news, Caleb knew me as the guy who would show up at the pool in uniform. As a teenager, he lifeguarded at the Moab aquatic center, where Wendy often took the kids on summer days. As often as I could, I'd swing by the pool on my lunch hour, just to say hi and get some time with them. Years later, after *he* ended up all over the news, Caleb let me know that he'd noticed my visits to the pool. It made an impression on him that I took time in the middle of the day to hang out with my family.

His dad, Craig Shumway, was a sergeant in the Moab Police Department. Caleb remembers where he was the night I was shot: at that high school production of *Fiddler on the Roof*. A couple of his friends were in the play, and he recalls how word of the shooting got out while people were still there. And he remembers the sight of his grim-faced father, suited up in his camo, long gun in hand, leaving the house to join the manhunt.

Caleb didn't follow his dad into law enforcement, but he did end up in uniform. In 2015, he joined the US Air Force Reserve—the 419 Fighter Wing, to be exact—where his duties included working on the weapons systems of F-35 fighter jets. He joined because he loves the Air Force and wanted to serve but also because the recruiter told him that if he signed on the dotted line, his student debt could be paid off.

Caleb signed, then treated himself to the near-inconceivable luxury of taking a semester of classes at Utah Valley without working a job at the same time, as he'd always done in the past. It was only then that he discovered "all the strings attached" to getting the Air Force to pay off his student debt. "I was like, well, that's not going to happen," he recalls. Thus, he found himself in the conundrum of needing to take classes to prevent his student loan debt from taking on interest while at the same time lacking the funds to enroll in those classes.

With increasing frequency, his thoughts drifted to me. Well, not to me, exactly, but to the $30,000 reward that had been offered "for information leading to the apprehension and/or recovery of the person" who shot me. That language comes from a press release issued by the FBI's Salt Lake City Division, which contributed $10,000 toward that bounty, as did the US Marshals Service and the Utah Department of Natural Resources. Gazing out from his mugshot, appearing sullen and resigned, is Arellano, forever forty in that photograph.

The failure of the manhunt to turn up Arellano fed oxygen to numerous theories and lines of speculation. Some believed that he ended up in the river and drowned. Others said he'd escaped into the desert, then lit out for parts unknown, a theory I found implausible considering he had no cell phone, food, or money. In my favorite far-fetched

Arellano scenario, the fugitive had somehow eluded that massive dragnet and made his way to Southern California, where he worked as a mechanic for a motorcycle gang.

I figured there was less than a 3 percent chance he was still alive. But that 3 percent was enough to prey on my mind every once in a while, making me wonder if my family and I were safe. Mostly, I didn't sweat it. My kids were different, however. Telling them there was only a very small chance that Arellano was still out there was a long, long way, I learned, from telling them there was *no* chance. When you're a kid, your mind leaps directly to the darkest possibility.

Caleb Shumway didn't think Arellano was alive. He'd followed my case with considerable interest because he knew me—at least to say hello to—and because his dad helped search for Arellano. Before Craig Shumway went into law enforcement, he was a uranium miner. "So we spent a lot of time hopping into old mine shafts," Caleb reminisces, "going under debris and through stuff. A couple rocks falling overhead was no biggy." Where some people are uncomfortable on the uneven surfaces of the high desert, the Shumways "don't even think about it," he says. Navigating canyons or jumping off ledges is second nature to them: "Some people go for a walk in the park; we climb cliffs."

Seven months after chancing upon those remains on Kyhv Peak, Caleb was home for Thanksgiving, hiking the Moab Rim Trail with friends. But a mere hike, as we've established, is too tame for Shumway. He needs to spice it up, challenge himself, make it an adventure, which is how he ended up in a field of boulders, often crawling on the ground through gaps between the rocks. That's when his mind took him to a different place. "I began to feel like I was searching for human remains," he says.

What came next was something akin to a vision. On that plateau one thousand feet over the river, he saw himself looking down from a raptor's vantage at that stunning and cruel topography below, the mesas and spires and bends in the river: "It was so weird. I was up high, looking through a bird's eyes, and there was a skull." There was zero doubt in his mind, descending the switchbacks and on the drive home, that the skull in his vision belonged to Arellano.

As he'd been drawn to Rock Canyon, he now felt a more powerful call. "There was something that kinda woke back up in me," he remembers, "a calling, or prompting, to go find that body."

Chapter 20

MOM POWER

A year had passed since the shooting, and I was back at work full time—mostly administrative, desk-bound duties, but I was back.

After we flew home from our Thanksgiving in the tropics, my supervisor, Tony White, talked me into driving up to Salt Lake for a fancy banquet hosted by the Utah Department of Natural Resources (DNR). People were inspired by my story and would enjoy meeting me, White told me. What he didn't tell me was that they planned to call me up on the dais and present me with the Executive Director's Choice Award for what I'd gone through in the previous year. It was a cool moment and a total surprise.

The next day, I had a meeting with Dave Harris, who coordinated the DNR's boating program. Harris offered me a promotion to assistant boating program manager. In that role I would work closely with commercial boating outfits on the Sevier, Green, Provo, Ogden, Weber, and Colorado Rivers—the Moab rafting companies I knew so well and others throughout the state. I'd also be involved in education, enforcement, rulemaking, and training. It was a great fit, squarely in my wheelhouse.

A small part of me was conflicted about returning to full duty. A little over a year after I was shot, members of the Weber Morgan Narcotics Strike Force conducted a nighttime raid on the Ogden, Utah, home of Matthew David Stewart, whose ex-girlfriend had told police he was growing pot in his basement. It turned out Stewart was a veteran who used the weed to treat his post-traumatic stress disorder, or PTSD. After police took down his door with a battering ram, Stewart, who'd been asleep, grabbed a handgun. In the ensuing gunfight, one officer was killed and five others wounded.

That was a dark day in our house as well, and Wendy and I questioned whether I should return to full duty—and carry a gun. I had qualms. But I loved the job and knew I could still do it well. I ran at the fear and spent much of that second year following my attack requalifying for law enforcement duties. This was not a slam dunk. There were a lot of people above me who needed to be convinced beyond the shadow of a doubt that I was fit to return to my old job. I went through the three-day Basic Field Training Officer Course again and passed comfortably. I submitted to a battery of psychological evaluations. Looking back on it, I'd say my supervisors were mean to me—in the kind of tough-love way Wendy sometimes had been. They wanted to make sure I was ready to come back. I was, and I did—even though I had very few law enforcement duties in the new gig.

I spent a lot of time driving between Moab and Salt Lake City, a lot of time at a desk, and a lot of time on the water. But where I did not spend time was in the backcountry, solo, doing law enforcement. That was a gift to me but more so to my family.

I've described my convalescence and rehab—my comeback—as a journey back to myself. I didn't realize it in real time, but Wendy was on a similar journey back to herself. With each baby step I took away from dependency, her burden, though still heavy, was made incrementally lighter. With each milestone—*he can dress himself . . . feed himself . . . go to the bathroom on his own; he can work two hours . . . a half day . . . a full day*—she reclaimed more of her identity, which had become collateral damage from the night I was ambushed.

How do I mean that? Wendy sacrificed deeply to help me recover. That's inspiring but not surprising. It's who she'd always been. Selflessness, showing up for others, had long been her default mode. "She didn't have to learn that lesson or how to be in that role," says her friend Christy Calvin. "She was already that person." It was ingrained in her identity.

But the service then asked of her was unlike any she'd ever performed. For a week or so, my life hung in the balance, which tends to ratchet up the trauma, even for notoriously cool customers such as Wendy. Later, it fell to her to care for me while at the same time caring for our children. She would also be called upon, from time to time, to manage members of our extended family—and our friend groups, including close friends but sometimes extending to more casual acquaintances and folks who didn't know us that well but nonetheless felt moved to show up at the hospital or, later on, our house. No wonder the woman felt completely overwhelmed. No wonder there were tense interludes with some family members who forgot themselves at times and told Wendy in no uncertain terms that she was doing it wrong.

She was comfortable and happy in the service of others. But that service had been on her terms. This was not. This was a roiling stretch of chaos and uncertainty that went on for well over a year—getting markedly worse after I was discharged from the hospital. "You weren't even eating or pooping, for God's sake, and they sent you home to be cared for by Wendy, who was already caring for three children," declares our friend Janel Arbon. "Wendy, being Wendy, stepped up to the plate and did it. . . . And you know what? She's still tired."

Wendy, so used to pitching in—"always the one doing stuff for everyone else," notes Calvin—now found herself in need of help. That went against her independent grain. It irked her, as did the general public's seemingly insatiable desire for details and updates, rooted in genuine concern though it may have been. "It made her angry and uncomfortable to be in that situation," Calvin adds. "A lot of it was the stress."

Seeing the glaring need, her friends stepped in, providing caretaking for the caretaker. They ran interference, served as gatekeepers. They accompanied her on walks, on bike rides, to lunch. They would take our kids for an hour. What they did not tend to do—my feelings are not hurt by this—was ask for a "Brody update." They were asking how *she* was doing. "Because she needed that venting time, that walking time," recalls Jennifer Taylor. "Or she was going to blow a gasket."

With her volunteer work at school and prolific coaching of youth swimming and soccer teams, Wendy had earned a reputation as a quiet leader in the community and a pillar of strength, both physical and mental. It's not like she curated that reputation; Wendy doesn't much care what anyone thinks of her. (Have I mentioned that one of her creative outlets was making these cool *3:10 to Yuma*-looking coffins from wood scraps she'd find around town? The finished products are more objets d'art than actual coffins you would bury someone in. But give her time.)

That was, nonetheless, her identity. At least it was until I got shot, and she became known almost exclusively as the wife of the ranger who was ambushed and left for dead. "It's difficult for Wendy to be known or have people looking at her," says Calvin. "Before this happened, that's not who she was or who she wants to be." Wendy grew weary and, yes, resentful of the new identity fate had forced upon her.

Time passed; I improved. In fits and starts, so gradually we often failed to notice it was happening, we edged back toward what might be described as "normal life"—and our old identities. Let me be more precise: I'd say we returned to new and improved versions of ourselves.

For a solid year, we were sorely and repeatedly tested, but we emerged from those trials more unified, a stronger couple, a better team—much the same way Gandalf the

Gray is forced to wrestle with the Balrog, then "pass through fire and death" before he emerges, more powerful than ever, as Gandalf the White.

I'd always talked a good game about putting family first, and I did an OK job backing those words up. After coming so close to missing out on the rest of their lives, I've put a higher priority on walking that walk. I am more devoted to my wife and our marriage. It's the least I could do, right? I took inventory of things that were inserting space between us and got rid of some of them. We no longer have satellite or cable television in our living room, for instance. I used to be the guy who sat down, unconsciously grabbed the remote, and put on a football game. Instead of me watching the tube, now I'm much more likely to have a substantial conversation with Wendy or one of the kids. We interact. It's meaningful. And each morning—well, most mornings—I will ask myself what I can do to make Wendy's day better.

It's not like we've ascended to some level of higher consciousness where the tribulations of everyday life can't reach us. We're still in the hurly-burly of the world. Money's still tight. Job pressure doesn't really ever go away. Each of our kids brings us singular joys . . . and challenges. The difference is that at this point in our journey, having survived what we've survived, we're less likely to stress out too much—"freak out," as Wendy would put it—over small-bore problems. What I tell people when I'm giving my speech is "When it seems like the sky is falling, you need to relax and realize it's just the roof caving in."

As the months and years ticked past, the shooting receded, got smaller and smaller in the rearview mirror. It took up less bandwidth. It was safely in the past. And then it wasn't.

Not quite two years after the incident, Jayde started kindergarten. I'd been attacked in mid-November when she was three years old. Now with summer giving way to autumn in Moab, leaves on the aspen and cottonwoods turning a vibrant yellow, the change of seasons awakened something deep within her.

PTSD is a serious psychological problem once thought to afflict only soldiers returning from war. According to Dr. David Hill, a North Carolina–based pediatrician and national authority on child development, "any really significant traumatic event or series of events can lead to PTSD, even in young children." "Really frightening, really awful events"—such as one's father nearly being shot to death—"leave an imprint on our brains," which respond "by becoming hypervigilant and hyperworried . . . or by being ready to respond to any trigger with violence of our own, or with panic of our own."

The PTSD lay dormant in Jayde for two years. When it awakened, "it kicked her butt," recalls Wendy. It wasn't always clear what triggered her, but she suffered a series of panic attacks at the elementary school. The poor thing would try to run out of the school building, but the doors locked her in. Wendy would arrive and be standing helplessly on the other side of the door, watching Jayde scream and pound on the glass, trying to get out. It was brutal for our little girl, brutal for Wendy, brutal for all of us.

We knew where Jayde's emotions were coming from but struggled to find ways to help her. Wendy had taken Stryder and Jayde to see therapists before but never found one who was a fit for them. "We tried two or three different counselors," Wendy remembers, "and we would come home angrier than when we left."

Jayde has always been the sriracha in our family—"a fireball of energy," as Wendy once put it in a Christmas card, "as fierce with her love and hugs as she is with her temper." Her PTSD was fueled by a generalized anger—rage, really—at a world in which such an awful thing could've happened to her Brody. The change of seasons set her off. But she had other triggers: the smell of disinfectant or other sights and sounds that might remind her of a hospital. Her periodic panic attacks continued for several years. And then Wendy found Antje (pronounced "Ontia").

A friend of ours going through a complicated adoption process told us about Antje Rath, a counselor based in Moab. Antje had helped that family a great deal. Wendy got Jayde in to see Antje, who told her, basically, "I'll be your friend. You can tell me whatever you want, and I won't tell your mom." "I was kind of nervous," Wendy remembers, "but I was like, if it helps, go for it."

To help Jayde with her anger, Antje had her build cities of Legos—and then destroy them. "How did therapy go?" we might ask, and Jayde would reply, "I built a giant city, then I took a bat to it." Whatever they were doing and talking about, it worked. Even after she became Jayde, Destroyer of Worlds, she didn't get better all at once. But she did get better, gradually, until the anger was under control and the panic attacks stopped. (Antje was also a big help to Stryder, who was working through his own delayed PTSD around the same time.)

Another tool Antje shared with Jayde was a series of breathing exercises that calmed her and sometimes pulled her back from the edge. When Jayde was in second grade, her teacher learned about those breathing exercises and how helpful they were to her. Rather than make Jayde feel singled out, the teacher would have the entire class participate in those exercises. That teacher was Jill Tatton, a ministering angel from an earlier chapter.

Aware that Jayde loves rocks and crystals, Antje instructed Wendy to pick up some beautiful and arresting samples at a shop downtown. Wendy's next job was to "carry them around," she recalls, in order to "charge them up with Mom Power." Fortified with those charged rocks in her pockets, Jayde would venture forth to school, where the Mom Power helped her feel connected and supported. As Wendy remembers, "She'd come home and say, 'OK, Mom, this one's getting low; can you charge it for me?'"

She carried those rocks for at least four years. By then, much of her PTSD had abated. What never disappeared, however—and this applied to all of us—was this nagging, gnawing desire to learn the fate of Lance Leeroy Arellano, who had disappeared into the badlands that memorable night and was never seen again.

Chapter 21

"WE GOT OUR GUY"

Caleb Shumway's compulsion, his calling to locate the remains of Lance Arellano, only increased throughout 2015—as did his student debt-related stress. He started talking to his buddies back in Orem about it, he says, "as kind of a serious joke, at first." As time passed, he ventured farther out onto that limb. "I don't know where I got off," he says, "but I was mentioning it to people, quite vocally, saying, 'Hey, there's this bounty on this body, and I'm gonna go find it.'" By putting his plan out in the world that way, he was cutting off his own escape routes, all possibility of retreat, forcing himself to follow through.

When he got home for Christmas break that year, he sat down with his parents and shared his plan: he intended to spend the next two weeks searching for Arellano. Or what remained of him. His dad reminded him that over two hundred law enforcement agents had failed in that task, and they had bloodhounds and helicopters. In the five years since the manhunt ended, hundreds of amateur trackers had also combed the search area, all in vain. Caleb was undeterred. "I am *going* to find this body," he told his parents. "This is my desert, and if anybody is going to find him, it will be me."

Then he added, "I'm good at finding weird stuff in weird places."

His parents forbade him to embark on the quest alone. Not a problem: Caleb had recruited his fifteen-year-old brother, Jarom, selling the mission as a fun-filled adventure and downplaying the certainty of physical discomfort—it was December, so there would be cold rain and snow—and the drudgery of scouring the desert for days on end. Jarom knew he was being spun but still jumped at the chance to hang out and bond with his big brother.

Before heading out, Caleb had picked his father's brain. Craig Shumway strongly believed that Arellano was still somewhere within that squeezed-down four-square-mile search area just north and east of Caveman Ranch. The fugitive had found a deep cave, Craig believed, then curled up and died.

It was Caleb's intention to hit the road "at the break of dawn" on Wednesday, December 22, and put in a full day of searching "the potash area" around where Arellano's car and possessions were found. He and his brother left the house at 1 p.m. sharp. Yes, they were running a bit behind schedule. But they were very well rested.

Where would they look? Caleb had already put much thought into establishing the boundaries of their search. Their easternmost boundary was the Colorado River, which runs very chilly in November—as Arellano probably knew. Searchers had repeatedly scoured the riverbank, never finding his footprints. The second boundary was the dirt road originating at Caveman Ranch and following a dusty course west and north in the direction of some evaporation ponds used to process mined potash.

One of the first principles of looking for a fugitive, Caleb points out, is that eventually, they must leave footprints. Hundreds of trackers had looked for any sign of Arellano's footprints south of that road and found none. That was their second border.

The final leg of the search triangle wasn't as self-evident. After ditching his Pontiac, Arellano had walked south in the direction of a "wash," a shallow channel that follows the contours of the land, allowing water to flow (or wash) from higher elevations to lower—in this case, from the elevated spot where he left his car down to the river. There was evidence of Arellano entering the wash but no evidence of him ever leaving it. They decided the wash would form the third leg of the search boundary.

The brothers didn't find their rhythm right away. The first thing they did, after establishing their final boundary, was to investigate a group of caves just *outside* the boundary. "There were some caves—caves in this case meaning rocks that had fallen in on each other and created little pockets—that a sneaky person might potentially be drawn to. So we snooped around up in there," Caleb recollects. "Then we got distracted by an old mining camp. And *then* we got back on task and went back to our search grid." Starting from a fixed point on the grid, they would pick a spot at the end of the search boundary and walk a straight line toward it. Every notable feature—overhangs, caves, cracks in rocks—was searched and cleared. Then they'd move over fifty feet and start again.

After several solid hours of searching, with dusk now upon them—this was one day after the winter solstice, the second-shortest day of the year—they trudged back to the car. "I felt a little discouraged," Caleb later wrote. "I was so determined to find this guy. But I doubted myself." He wanted very much to enlist the aid of his father. "But if I wanted the reward to be valid, I would have to do this on my own. I said a prayer before I went to bed, and my nerves were calm."

The forecast for December 23 in Moab was not promising: mixed snow and rain and temperatures hovering around freezing. Undaunted, the brothers Shumway prepared to seize the day, this time leaving the house well before noon (11:38 a.m.). By now a well-oiled machine, they moved methodically through their search grid, stopping for lunch around 2 p.m. Caleb was already getting restless, antsy. "We were going back and forth and not getting any results, and I got a little impatient," he remembers.

The sector they'd just cleared was straightforward—what he calls one of the "less likely" areas, meaning they probably wouldn't find any skeletons there, but they had to clear it to check it off the list. So he made an executive decision. Rather than proceed to yet another "less likely" area, they would jump ahead to more promising ground.

But where? Sitting on a ridge of rock with his brother, trying to quiet his mind, to find the still place, he sent a question out into the universe: "I just really kind of reached out with my soul and asked, Where *is* he?" The answer came back to him: *Right in front of you.*

Arellano's last known tracks, indicating his movement away from the stashed rifle and backpack, had been found at the far end of the elevated, complicated riot of red rock we dubbed the Dragonback Hammerhead—whose cephalofoil-shaped sandstone head was about ten meters to their left as they finished their sandwiches. "Let's get in there," Caleb said to his brother, pointing to the far side of that formation. "Let's go there now." So they cut the line, moving to a spot that had been at the end of their search grid.

It wasn't an original idea. Five years earlier, a veritable cavalry of law enforcement agents had focused their search efforts on this same complex formation. Mindful of that, the brothers climbed to its steepest, most rugged reaches, clambering over boulders and descending into crevices that would've confounded many of the troopers and deputies who'd come before.

Working from high to low, they discovered numerous caves, more than Caleb had expected. The brothers stuck to their system: if the beam of a flashlight could not find the back of the cave, Caleb would venture in to clear it while Jarom remained at the entrance, prepared to summon assistance—or, more realistically, shout encouragement—if his sibling found himself in combat with a mountain lion or coyote.

Emerging from a cave at one point, Caleb saw a falcon alight from its hiding place on the far side of a cliff. His mind returned to that indelible moment on the Moab Rim Trail—to the bird's-eye view, the skull, the clarion call to come find this body. "When I saw the falcon," he says, "it was kind of a callback to that vision, a reassurance that, OK, you're in the right spot."

They pressed on. Maneuvering his way around a ledge, he dropped into the most extensive cave they'd yet found. Awaiting him was a surprisingly large volume of coyote scat but no fugitive. "This was strange," he later noted. "A coyote had used this cave for a significant amount of time, but it was in an abnormal location for hunting and scavenging."

Around 4 p.m., with just over an hour of sunlight remaining, the brothers decided to call it a day. "We'd been out in the elements, in December, all day," Caleb remembers. "Mentally, physically, emotionally, we were done." First, they'd have to get down off the dragon's back.

Crossing over the spine to begin his descent, Caleb's eye was drawn to a kind of inlet in the rocks—he describes it as a "cove"—they hadn't noticed before. "Even though we were trying to get home," he recalls, "in my mind, I just picked to beeline it to the back of that cove." Jarom was cool with the detour, which was "pretty normal to our kind of adventuring," he says. "Obviously we were cold, tired and hungry, but I was just happy to be out there, hanging with my brother. Also, it was on our way to the car."

As they approached the cove and the cave they presumed to be beneath it, Jarom stayed high, on a taller section of rock. Caleb dropped down off those boulders,

"WE GOT OUR GUY"

searching for easier access. As they drew closer, Caleb heard his younger brother's voice from above: "Hey—a bone!" Bounding up to join him, Caleb peered into the hole where his brother was pointing. "The bone was just sitting right in the center, light shining down on it, like it had been placed there," he remembers.

Determined ranchers have long run cattle in the Moab Valley, so there are a few cow bones scattered in the desert. But not up here. Not on the Dragonback Hammerhead. This wasn't a cow bone. Caleb, who knew about human skeletons, suspected he was looking at someone's clavicle.

Lowering himself into the hole, he placed one hand next to the bone, to provide scale, then snapped a picture with his phone. One of the hats his father wore for the Moab Police Department was that of medical examiner. He looked forward to his analysis of whether they were looking at a human or animal bone.

After getting that photo, Caleb looked around the hole. That's when he saw a weathered yellow bag: "So I go to pull the bag out, and it rips open. And I see a gun mag and a pistol inside the bag. . . . And at that moment I glance off to the left, and my eyes peer into the deep, dark blackness of this cave, and just as clear as daylight, my mind was very aware there was a body back in that hole." Awash in adrenaline, Caleb catapulted out of the hole. "Jarom, we found him!"

Feeling "one thousand percent confident," Caleb now wanted to head home. He was in no rush to lay eyes on another skeleton. Nor did he want his fifteen-year-old brother to see one. They would return with sheriff's deputies in the morning. Caleb snapped more photos, they marked the location, and then they headed back to the car.

On the morning of December 24, at the end of his fifth year on the job, Grand County Sheriff Steve White got a call from Sergeant Craig Shumway. "You want to solve the Arellano case?" asked Craig. The sheriff allowed that he did, very much.

Craig and Caleb met at the sheriff's office with White and two investigators. They drove north out of town, left on Potash Road, and past the turnoff to Poison Spider Mesa, where five years, one month, and five days earlier, Lance Arellano had last been seen alive.

Sheriff White took a right on the dirt road just past Caveman Ranch and parked nearby. That discombobulated Caleb just a little. He was used to approaching the search area from the other direction. Up on that rock formation, all eyes on him, he missed the cave on his first pass-through, walked right by it. "Coming in from the new angle confused me," he later wrote in his official report. But after spying the bone, he found the cave.

At this point, Caleb felt certain his work was done. The professionals would take it from there—locating the remains and packing them out in the body bag they'd brought along for the occasion. Caleb would secure the bounty, extend to his brother a fair cut, then pay off his student loans. Life was good. But there were problems down in the cave. The investigators couldn't find a body.

"WE GOT OUR GUY"

One of them emerged and asked Caleb, "Are you sure he's down here?"

"Yep. A hundred percent sure," he replied.

After searching a while longer, the officer came back out. "He's not in there."

"At this point I'm sweating," Caleb recalls. "I just drove these guys out here on Christmas Eve on a wild goose chase, is how they're seeing it." He dropped down into the cave himself and directed them to that recess on the left, the dark place his eyes were drawn to the day before. Pointing to that aperture and the black chamber beyond, he asked the deputies, "Did you go all the way back in there?" They had not, nor were they eager to do so. Sliding through that crevice was going to prove a difficult feat for the investigators, who by this time in their lives "had acquired adult physiques," recalled Caleb in a masterpiece of diplomacy.

At least one of them expressed concern about a "loose rock" in the roof of the cave, which might fall and injure them. When it became apparent that none of them intended to go back there, Caleb switched from spectator to participant.

Shumway is a trim young man, and it was a squeeze even for him. As his chest passed through the opening, he remembers, "There was maybe half an inch between the top of the rock over me and the rock I was sliding on." On the far side of that gap, the ground dropped off. Standing again, Caleb tilted his head forward and, for the first time, saw the body in the beam of his headlamp. He began calling out the parts he saw:

"I got a shoe!"

"I got ribs and a spine!"

There were pants and a belt and hiking boots.

He emerged from the side cave, describing to deputies in fuller detail what he'd seen. "We got our guy," Sheriff White declared. And now they needed to get their guy, literally, by bagging his body after documenting the scene with photographs. The problem? None of the deputies believed they'd be able to squeeze through that slender portal.

Caleb piped up. "I'll take the pictures and collect the body; just give me the camera bag and gloves," he said, according to the report he filed with the sheriff's office. The older men were hesitant to take him up on that offer, he recalls. Then Sheriff White, noting that it wasn't an active crime scene, decided they could accept his help.

Back into that close, tight crypt went Caleb. Arellano had passed away in his sleeping bag, which had since been "chewed open by coyotes," Caleb recounts. "He had some food down there, so it looks like he tried to eat and stay warm but didn't survive." After taking "a lot of pictures," he passed the camera up, put on latex gloves, and commenced transferring the remains to the body bag. The space was so cramped and enclosed, there wasn't room for him to even squat beside the skeleton. With the job half done, he passed the loaded bag through the narrow passage to the other men. It was soon returned to him empty, and he kept working. In a second, smaller backpack, he found a .40-caliber pistol, the gun Arellano shot me with. He handed that up to the sheriff.

Caleb had dreamt the night before that a skull was staring him in the face. In the dream and afterward, he knew whose skull it was. "Actually, it was more of a nightmare," he recounts. "There was this sense of fear that came with it." To avoid that scenario in real life, he "pivoted" the skull so that it faced away from him, then placed it in a smaller bag and handed it up.

After searching the space for smaller bones that had been dispersed, he passed the sleeping bag up the hole. "I went right behind it," he wrote. "I have no desire to go into that cave again. After 90 minutes I stepped back into the sunlight."

Two weeks later, the Utah Medical Examiner's Office announced that it had used dental records to positively identify the body as that of Lance Leeroy Arellano.

Yes, Caleb succeeded where a far larger force of professional law enforcement officers had failed. A modest young man, he makes a key distinction: "They were in a manhunt. They didn't know if the guy was alive. They had to move with much more caution." Without the threat of an attempted murderer popping out of a hole to do them harm, the Shumway brothers "moved with a lot more freedom," says Caleb. "We could climb over boulders and gaps and search all the way to the back of the caves, without fear." If authorities *had* discovered Arellano's lair five years earlier, there's a good chance more officers would have been shot, Caleb believes.

From Arellano's hideaway in that smaller chamber, he could see the cave entrance through a narrow opening. In the smaller pack close to him was the Glock. "I never dropped the mag to see if it was loaded, but I would assume that he was ready. Thank goodness they didn't find him," says Caleb, who did collect the reward money, then paid down his student loans, after giving Jarom his cut.

I had a bunch of emotions when I got the news. In a way, I'm still processing them. We felt relief for ourselves and our children and immense gratitude to the Shumways and to everyone who'd helped in the search and the often frustrating five-year investigation. I felt a powerful sense of resolution, clarity, closure. In that respect, the news was a gift. But we felt no joy. I shot Arellano in defense of my own life. Once the gunfight was over, I never wished him dead. I didn't thirst for revenge, not even a little. Neither did Wendy.

His remains were discovered on Christmas Eve, five years to the day after I was released from St. Mary's. The timing transcended mere coincidence. It put us in mind of all the other remarkable, unlikely events—the strokes of fortune, major and minor, that wove through my story and, in some cases, kept me alive.

We had an excellent but somber Christmas. After the presents were unwrapped and mayhem subsided and Wendy got out for a run, I drove over to the Shumways' house. I needed to thank those two young men, especially Caleb, in person. Rather than describe our exchange, which I treasure, I invite you to read the final two paragraphs of his report:

> Christmas day. I got a call from the sheriff, he asked me if he could give my number to NBC. I thought it would

be fine. Just a bit later NBC called and wanted to do an interview on Christmas; I said we should be with our friends and family and that on the 26th I would do an interview at any time.

At 3:06 Brody Young came out and visited. He stepped into the door and looked into my eyes and thanked me. We sat down and talked about it all. He talked about how this was amazing for his family. He talked about how the previous day's news was the 5-year anniversary of coming home from the hospital after being shot 9 times. I thought finally his family can know for sure that they are safe. I was so humbled to be in his presence. For a while I had felt a little bit bad about being so focused on the bounty. But I realized why I was after the reward and it was only for good reasons and then I felt so much better. Brody is a man that speaks from much wisdom. We touched on the spirituality of it and we all recognize that God's hand was very deep in all of this.

What follows is our family's "statement to the press," issued jointly with Utah State Parks, following the discovery of the remains of Lance Arellano:

My wife, children and I wish to express our gratitude to the Shumway family for their dedicated and successful search efforts on this case. We wish to acknowledge the countless hours put in by the Grand and Weber

County Sheriff's Offices in this five-year investigation. We are grateful for Federal, State and local authorities who assisted in the initial search efforts and the ongoing investigation. Hundreds of officers and individuals spent countless hours searching the area. We appreciate their dedication and determination to bring this case to a close.

We are grateful for the first responders, ambulance crew, and medical staff at the Allen Memorial Hospital (now Moab Regional Hospital) for their quick response and treatment. We are indebted to the flight crew and the medical staff at St. Mary's Hospital in Grand Junction, Colorado. I wouldn't be alive without them. We also want to thank Mountain Land Physical Therapy for their tireless efforts in my complete rehabilitation.

There are so many others who have reached out and helped our family and while there are too many to individually recognize, we say thank you!

Our thoughts are with Lance Arellano's family, especially his mother and daughter. Five years of uncertainty is a long time. We hope this brings closure and allows them to move forward. We wish nothing but the best for them.

My family and I want everyone to know we have been and are extremely blessed. For many reasons, we were able to put the events of this unfortunate incident behind us several years ago. Due in large part to our faith, we have completely forgiven Lance Arellano. This event has strengthened us as a family and individually . . . and for that we are grateful.

With the help of those mentioned above along with many others, I have returned to work with Utah State Parks as a ranger with the boating program. My responsibilities include education, enforcement, navigation and policy making involving all types of boats. I continue to work as a Law Enforcement Ranger for the state of Utah. I'm proud to wear the badge again. I love my job! I enjoy serving the public and feel satisfaction in helping those I contact. I look forward to meeting you as you enjoy the great state of Utah!

On December 31, 2015, Sena Taylor Hauer wrote this in a column for the *Moab Times-Independent* titled "Closure and Peace":

I think we can all rest a little more easily knowing that the remains of Brody's assailant have been found. . . . Brody has proved to be a remarkable survivor, and he has been back on the job for quite some time. His wife, Wendy, held up under the most trying of circumstances, and through it all has shown herself to be one of the most generous volunteers in our community, most notably with our youth swim teams.

I've been told that Wendy garnered more votes for this year's Chamber of Commerce Citizen of the Year than any other individual. The Youngs are a fine family.

EPILOGUE

My mentor and longtime supervisor, Lieutenant Tony White, retired in December 2019 after a distinguished thirty-year career. I threw my hat in the ring to replace him and was promoted to lieutenant before he left. Like White, I'm now a certified firearms instructor. While not as forceful as he was, I put just as much emphasis on the importance of training—albeit in my own ex-hippie way.

On a sunny September morning in 2023, I took some out-of-town friends to visit the decrepit shell of Allen Memorial Hospital, which by that time had been closed for twelve and a half years. Bearing west on 400 North—that's the name of the road, not a specific address—we saw the spire of a modest LDS church, one of two in town, and then the weather-beaten wooden walls of the Snake Oil Coffee Company. There on the next block, set back on a lot of overgrown weeds, boarded up, graffiti tagged, and otherwise vandalized, was the building where a cast of local heroes helped me cheat death.

We got out of the car and milled around. The last time I'd been in this parking lot, I got a glimpse of the sky as they wheeled me from the ambulance bay into the ER. The hospital was clearly off limits, and that was fine by me. I hadn't been inside since that November night and wasn't feeling any kind of pull to go there now.

Feeling rather more adventurous was my friend Kim, who walked right up to the wooden front door and pushed it open a couple feet. Turning sideways, she ventured in, followed by her seventy-something ex-cop father, Gary, who didn't seem especially concerned as he remarked, "I hope this isn't breaking and entering."

We stepped into a postapocalyptic morass of Sheetrock scraps, exposed pipe, and busted glass crunching underfoot. On the registration desk, a tagger had spray-painted "Welcome to Sin City." I'd been rushed past that desk and into Room A—the critical room where nurses somehow pushed the entire contents of their blood bank into me in less than half an hour, much of it through the hole Phil Mosher drilled in my tibia.

Among the refuse on the floor was an old jigsaw, its blade bent and rusted. "There's the saw they were gonna use on your leg," said Gary, who noticed that my attention was elsewhere. I wasn't saying much. I was time traveling.

"How are you doing right now?" he asked, checking in on me.

"It's weird," I told him. "I can hear everyone's voices." I was hearing Phil and his fellow EMT, Michelle Steele. I was imagining once again the faces of ER doc Pat Scherer and Wendy, so determined to be brave but clearly scared. There were nurses Matt McCune and Annie Relph, who would meet

EPILOGUE

with us the following evening, September 19, 2023. I was gathering material for this book and recorded the conversation.

Annie shared that she'd been an RN for about a year the night they wheeled me in. "Yeah, that was my first gunshot wound. And I was thinking, *Holy s—, we're doing this right now.*" She was an excellent nurse, flawless and so cool under pressure. Annie remembered that the old hospital lacked a "mass transfuser," so they pushed blood in me the old-fashioned way, squeezing the bags, one after another. They stabilized me and put me on the chopper, and then it was someone else's turn to save my life.

We asked Annie to assess the ER's performance that night. "I'm looking at the resources we call to a trauma now," she replied, "compared to the resources we had for your trauma." She paused, then concluded, "We kicked ass." She was serious but had to smile in that moment, because she'd made all of us laugh.

The conversation meandered to Annie's upbringing in Wyoming and the summers she spent in Moab, lifeguarding at the water park owned by her aunt and uncle, Diane and Bob Norman. "That place was awesome," I recalled. "It wasn't awesome when there was a flash flood and we had to shovel mud out of the pool," Annie remarked. "We did not love that."

Eventually, we returned to the subject of my near-death experience. By this point in the conversation, we were more relaxed. "This is really personal," I shared, "but I got a taste of the other side" after being shot.

"Do you remember?" she asked me. "You don't have to talk about it if you don't want to."

I was fine talking about it. "I didn't see a light," I told her. "It was more of a supercalm, painless feeling. Peaceful. Comforting." It was similar to my dream in the ICU of being on that train to Plymouth Rock, surrounded by family. "The other side's not so bad," I told her.

She nodded and took that in, then observed, "When it's your time, it's your time." Then she added, "And when it's not your time, it's not your time," referring to the fact that I'd survived the shooting.

Annie was killed in a car wreck four and a half months later, hit head-on by a driver who crossed into her lane on Highway 191, south of Moab. Her preteen son, Ledger, was critically injured. The driver of the other car, a fifty-year-old man, died of his injuries as well. She was forty-six and had been the director of nursing at Moab Regional Hospital since 2019. That year, she was named Utah's Emergency Nurse of the Year. Informed of the city's plan to honor her by driving her through Moab on a fire truck, she put a quick end to that nonsense, declaring, "I'm not doing that!" Of course she relented, even donning a red cape and tiara for the occasion. She left behind four children and her husband, Josh.

Her death rocked me and many others in our town. It struck me as a cruel irony and unfair that I'm still around while this vital, upbeat woman who played a key role in keeping me alive—in keeping countless members of our community alive—is gone. It left me wondering, not for the

EPILOGUE

first time, about our Maker's plan for each of us. I returned to questions I've often asked in the wake of surviving that ambush: *Why was I spared? What's my purpose?*

My purpose, as I see it, is to maximize and make the most of the second chance I was given—to live a meaningful life, like Annie Relph, and make a difference. Part of that is sharing this story in hopes that it might inspire someone who is struggling or up against long odds and thinking of giving up to work the problem, stay in the fight.

In moments of crisis, we fall to the level of our training. If you're not trained in self-defense, consider it. And if you are, take the training seriously. It might save your life. And if you're bearing a grudge, I get it. You've been wronged. You have the *right* to feel aggrieved! But if it's an old grudge, or even a new one, think about setting it aside for a while, and see how that feels. Consider forgiveness.

Why am I still alive? That's a complex, unknowable mystery. On the other hand, it couldn't be simpler or clearer. I fought for my life so I could spend the balance of my years with Wendy and our children, who appeared to me as I lay dying, in extremis.

Here's the thing about almost dying: it's clarifying. You end up making a list—at least a mental list—of things you'll do if you get a second chance. I felt called to prioritize my wife and children. My family. The bonds between the five of us, stout to begin with, are now even stronger.

It is immutable, a law of nature, that sons and daughters will rebel against their parents. But in a felicitous twist that might well qualify as this book's tenth miracle, each of our three children is passionate about whitewater rafting. They love running the river and—if I may brag a little—are quite skilled at it: reading the water and steering clear of most hazards. Even as they are now teenagers, commanded by their DNA to avoid the company of their parents, they happily join us on rafting trips.

And so this story, which began near the banks of the Colorado, comes to a close on the same river, with the five of us shouting and laughing our way through the whitewater. The grim events of a certain autumn night are far behind us and getting smaller. Our eyes are downriver, in the direction of our next adventure.